THE
Fruitful Family

THE
Fruitful Family

John Githiga

ReadersMagnet, LLC

The Fruitful Family
Copyright © 2020 by John Githiga

Published in the United States of America
ISBN Paperback: 978-1-951775-53-7
ISBN eBook: 978-1-951775-54-4

All rights reserved. No part of this publication may be reproduced, stored in a retrieval system or transmitted in any way by any means, electronic, mechanical, photocopy, recording or otherwise without the prior permission of the author except as provided by USA copyright law.

The opinions expressed by the author are not necessarily those of ReadersMagnet, LLC.

ReadersMagnet, LLC
10620 Treena Street, Suite 230 | San Diego, California, 92131 USA
1.619.354.2643 | www.readersmagnet.com

Book design copyright © 2020 by ReadersMagnet, LLC. All rights reserved.
Cover design by Ericka Obando
Interior design by Shemaryl Tampus

OTHER BOOKS BY THE AUTHOR

The Spirit in the Black Soul

CHRIST AND ROOTS:
Jesus as Revealed in the Bible and the African Traditional Religions

INITIATION AND PASTORAL PSYCHOLOGY:
Toward African Personality Theory

MINISTRY TO ALL NATIONS:
Practical Theology of Mission and Church Planting

70 SERMONS:
Liturgical Preaching

GOSPEL TO ALL NATIONS:
Preaching from the Lectionary

THE SECRETS OS SUCCESS IN MARRIAGE

25 SECRETS OF SUCCESS IN MARRIAGE

30 SECREATS OF SUCCESS IN MARRIAGE:
A Book for Premarital and Marriage Counseling

SYSTEMATIC THEOLOGY:
An Introduction to the African Theological Voice

CONTENTS

Acknowledgement 9
About the Author 11
About the Book 13

Chapter 1: Introduction 15
Chapter 2: Planting the Seed in Children 19
Chapter 3: Autonomy 3-6 Years 27
Chapter 4: Industry and Work 7-12 Years 30
Chapter 5: Self Identity 13-20 Years 32
Chapter 6: Young Adulthood 21-39 35
Chapter 7: Generativity and Creation 40-55 Years 37
Chapter 8: Old Age 40
Chapter 9: The Effect of the Names on Personality 42
Chapter 10: Seven Fundamentals for Fruitful Family 59
Chapter 11: Fruitfuness Golden Anniversary 64
Chapter 12: Nurture Your Best Self 67
Chapter 13: Avoid All Couses of Failure in Marriage 70
Chapter 14: Family In A Technological Society 87
Chapter 15: Division of Labor in the Family 91
Chapter 16: The Antistructure-Nararanja 121

Chapter 17: The Structure 126
Chapter 18: Lostness 130
Chapter 19: Pain 139
Chapter 20: Betrayal 155
Chapter 21: The Tree of God 157
Chapter 22: The Great Mother 164
Chapter 23: The Great Father 169
Chapter 24: We Are the Fruits of the Saints 175
Chapter 25: Conclusion 178

ACKNOWLEDGEMENT

We are most grateful to Dr. Glen and the Rev. Sue Sanborn for proof reading the book, To Dr David Brister, Mary Githiga and June Wambui and Rehema Njeri Githiga for their support. And to all the Students and Alumni of ANCCI University for their insights and All ANCCI for their prayer. May God richly bless you.

ABOUT THE AUTHOR

Dr. Githiga is Chancellor at ANCCI University, former chaplain and faculty at West Texas A&M University, Grambling State University, and instructor at Pensacola Junior College, Head of the Department of Pastoral Theology at St. Paul's University, founder and first President of the African Association for Pastoral Study and Counseling. He is a graduate from Church Army College, St. Paul's United Theological College, Makerere University, the University of the South, Vanderbilt University and the International Bible Institute and Seminary. He holds Dip.Th, M.Div, D.Min, DRE and D.D. He is married to the Rev. Dr. Mary Githiga.

ABOUT THE BOOK

Fruitful Family observes and discussed the face of Jesus in the international infants and children and discusses the importance of planting the seed of the gospel in all developmental stages. It discusses the of names and titles on personality it discusses the fundamentals of fruitful family and gives guidance on how to develop the best self so as to bear much fruits. It draws counseling insights from African and current personality theories the boo great for personal growth, Christian Counseling and family therapy based on Christian Principle.

CHAPTER 1

INTRODUCTION

The subject on **fruitful family** is of vital importance since the subject appears in the opening chapter and the closing chapter of the Bible. In creation story we read: "and then God said, 'let the land produce vegetation seed bearing plants and the tree on the land that **bear fruits with seed** in it according their various kinds. And it was so. The land produced vegetation plants bearing fruits with seeds according to their kinds. And God saw that it was good." Genesis 11, 1–12. After creating Adam and Eve, God blessed them and said to them: "Be fruitful and increase in number: fill the earth and subdue it. Rule over the fish of the sea and the bird of the air and every living creature that moves in the ground. Then God said, I give you **every seed–bearing plant in it**" the face of the whole earth and every tree that has fruit with seed in it. They will be your for food. And to all the beasts of the earth and all the birds of the air and all the creature that moves on the ground-everything that has the breath of life in it-I give every green plant for food. And it was so. And God saw that everything he has made, and it was very good. (Genesis 1:28–31)

The last chapter of the Bible tells us that the Apostle John saw the fruit bearing tree. Down in the middle of the great gate of the city, on each side of the river stood the tree of life, **bearing twelve crops of fruits**, yielding its fruits every month. And the leaves of the tree are for the heeling of the nations. No longer will there be a cure. And the throne of God and the lamb will be in the city. Revelation 22:1–3 Not very one will qualify for the fruits of the tree of God in the city of God, As a human being you were created with freedom choice. Each decision you make leads to either fruitful or fruitless life. At the end of all things, you will reap what you have planted. The seer puts it this way: "Let him who do wrong continue to do wrong, let him who is vile continue to be vile; let him who does right continue to do right, let him who is holy continue to be holy. Behold, I am coming soon. My reward is with me and I will give everyone according what he has done. I am alpha and Omega, the First and the Last and beginning and end. To prepare ourselves to the endless joyous life we have to wash our robes, that we may have right to the tree of life and may go through the gates of the city of God. Outside the city of God are those who practice magic, sexually immoral, the murderers, the idolaters and very one who loves and practice falsehood." Revelation 22:15.

Our Loving Savior tells us what to do to be fruitful. He indeed define the very meaning of being a Christian is to be fruitful. He puts it this way: I am the vine, you are the branches, if a man remain in me and I in him, he will bear much fruits, apart from me you can do nothing." John 15:5. All what you need to do is to let Christ in your life. He is closer to you that your nose is closed to your mouth. He says: "Here I am! I stand at the door and knock. If anyone hear my voice and open the door, I will come in and eat with him, and he with me." Revelation 3:20. When he comes in you immediately started bearing the fruit of the Holy Spirit which is "love, joy, peace, patient, kindness, goodness, faithfulness, gentleness and self-control." This is all what you need for a fruitful family. When you decide to lock him out of your life, you have decided to gratify the sinful nature. As the Apostle Paul put is: the acts of the sinful nature are obvious: sexual immorality, impurity, debauchery, idolatry, and witchcraft; hatred, discord, jealousy, fits of rage, selfish ambition, dissensions, factions and envy, drunkenness, orgies and the like. "Those who do things are not in the kingdom of God. They have opted to be useless to God, their family and the society. In our time people who have decided to be useless are taking drugs, alcohol and watching pornographic movies and photo. They impoverish the families and are dangerous to their neighbors. If you have been taking the useless road, you can make about turn. The first step is to accept that you are a sinner. For all have sinned and fallen shot of the glory of God, and are justified freely by his grace through the redemption that come by Christ Jesus. Roman 3:23. There is a real joy when we accept and confess our sin. the A post John puts it this way: If we claim to be without sin, we deceive ourselves and the truth is not in us, if we confess our sin, he is faithful and just and will forgive us our sin and to cleanse us from all unrighteousness. the good need is that when we confess our sin and let the Holy Spirit fill every fiber of our being, we are counted as thou we have never sinned. We start bearing the fruit of the Holy Spirit which is fundamental to a fruitful family.

Toe bear fruits the tree need strong roots. The Kikuyu proverbs says: The fruit bearing tree has strong roots. Roots are parents' teachers. The church need to prepare men and women to plant the seed. That is men and women fellowship should learn how to plant the seed in in children. It is from Sunday school teacher that I learned to sing all the books of the New Testament. We memorized key verses in the Bible like John 14:1–6. When Mary and I were in courtship, we faced strong fight. we were equipped by the motto of the Mothers Union which we were given by my mother in law: "I can do all things through Christ who strengthens me." And the word which we have memorized in Sunday Schooled: Let not your heart be troubled, you believe in God." Using these words our Loving Savior consistently reminded us that he is the way and the truth and the live.'

To bear much fruits we must eliminate weed which is spiritually unhealthy relationship. This include friends who only bear the fruits of the fresh. we must eliminate the weed which is any things that hinder or limit your spiritual growth. Weeds are the things that choke your relationship to Christ or that prevent you from further growth.

We must also cooperate with God's pruning in our lives. Pruning not only involves cutting off dead branches, but living ones as well in order to improve the shape of the plant and stimulate growth. Pruning is essential for increased productivity. **It's not optional**. If you're going to be productive in ministry, God will put you through times of pruning.

God prunes you for fruitfulness. In your life it's not only the dead wood that God cuts off; He also cuts back areas of success, EVEN areas that are bearing wonderful fruit. When He does this, you might struggle to understand why, but the reason is He is preparing you for even greater ministry.

Additionally, we must wait for the harves**t**. Growing fruit takes time. It doesn't come automatically. You don't plant a seed in the ground and harvest it the next day. It's common sense: seeds must be planted. You've got to cover them up with dirt, and then you wait and pray and expect growth. Just as a seed creates new life out of death, for you to be more effective in your ministry there's a dying to your old nature, a dying to your own desires and ambitions in the waiting process. Growth takes time, but don't give up. Stay plugged into Jesus Christ. Maybe you've been dormant in your ministry for some time. My prayer is that you'll give yourself to Christ, saying, "Lord, I want to work on these four things: cultivating my roots, eliminating the weeds, cooperating with Your pruning, and waiting for the harvest. God, I trust You with what I've planted, and I trust what I have sown will inevitably reap a harvest for You."

CHAPTER 2

PLANTING THE SEED IN CHILDREN

Mark report that people were bringing little children to Jesus but the disciple rebuked them, but Jesus said: "Let the little children come to me and do not hide them, for the kingdom of God belong to such as these." To the disciple's surprise, Jesus said that: "I tell you the truth, anyone who does not received the kingdom of God like a little child will never enter it." (Mark 10:13–16). Of course, the disciple were trying to safeguard the dignity of their Rabi for during those days the Rabi was not expected to teach children or interact with them. But Jesus took the children in his arms and blessed them.

So, our Master teaches us that the way to the Kingdom of God is being like little children. During the recent mission to Kenya, I had a great interest in observing children behavior. At the airplane, if they felt discomfort, the cried out loudly in such way that everybody will know about their filling. Arab, European, and African children were heaving the same.

Dr. John Githiga

YEAR 0-2 MOTHER IS THE FIRST

We will start from year 0-3. At this age the child learns the attribute of God from the mother. He learns that she is all powerful or powerless; She is loving or hateful; She control or grant me freedom She interacts with all human race and color and for that reason all human being are human being and you can have I Thou relationship with all races.

I had a most interesting interaction with one years old Egyptian baby at Frankford airport. I introduced myself to his mother who shook hand with me. And then Solomon held my fourth finger tightly and lovingly. He was, at the gut level saying, if my mother shakes your hand you are one of us. Even though the parents were Muslims the mother shared their faith and family history with me. She told me that Solomon is in Koran. Interestingly, not only that we shared the same humanity, but also the same ethnic, since I am a Kikuyu who are black Jews of Kenya who trace their origin to Solomon and Sheba the Ethiopian queen. Later on, I learned from my Sudanese student who lived in Egypt that the Arab mothers believe that a black man can bless their baby. Solomon didn't wait for the mother to bring him to me. So, he grumbled my index finger for the blessing.

Another rewarding episode took place at Chicago airport. An African American mother was hold a baby boy who cried as load as he could. The mother, instead of shouting at him, she put the baby at her breast and sooth the baby lovingly and tenderly. And gradually the baby kept quiet. As I was washing the drama, a voice said to me. She is a great mother and the child will grew to be a great man of God. The mother and her baby boarding the plain before me. As I was passing them the baby grumbled my thump tightly and gave me a winsome smile. At a gut level he was saying: "I will not let you go until you bless me." So, I laid my hands on him and said: "may the Lord bless you." He then let me go. On addition to asking for God's blessing the mother and the baby were breaking cultural barriers. They reminded me of an episode which tool place

The Fruitful Family

in Alabama where I was working as counselor at the youth camp which comprised of the inner-city youth. Meeting with African American teenager she asked: "Do you still eat people in African?" Before I responded the girl ran away for her security.

Interestingly, a nine months Mohamed became my hero as we were flying from Nairobi to Frankford. I had sat with his father who was speaking loudly and laughing with other Arab men. He avoided eye contact with me. As he was throwing his hand making me uncomfortable, I shouted: "Sir!" When he learned that I was black American he started gasping the American with other Arabs who were several rolls away from us. Six hour later little Mohamed was brought to the father by the mother. When the little angel was brought by the mother, he grumbled my fourth finger and gave me a winsome smile. He held my fourth finger for a long time even though the father didn't gave me eye contact. He has learned from his friendly mother that he can reach out to all human being-black, white, red and yellow. In contrast, I went to West Gate mall, Amarillo at children play ground. I sat next to a Mexican mother. I greeted her but she didn't respond or even look at me. Her Four-year daughter who was playing with other children ran to the mother complaining that another child has stepped on her and didn't' say sorry. I tried to reach out to the child to console her. But the little girl didn't even look at me. Being the father of many nations, I remember a critical episode with my Mexican parishioners. When I visited them, I found children in tear. The husband who was undocumented and was having problem getting job said: "Father John, I have to be strong for my family. My wife spent long hour with a dentist. She came home with lot of pain. Before entering the house, she was arrested and now she in a cell and I don't have money to bill her out." As he shared this story, his two children were crying over my shoulders. After consoling them I gave them the money for billing their mother out.

Another excited episode took place at Retina clinic where I was undergoing raiser surgery. As we were living, I saw two years old girl with her grandpa. The little angel looked at me fondly and then waive me goodbye. Even thou she was white she was saying to me: "May God be with you. You are also my grandpa."

As I was interacting with international children and parents, I had a dream in which I saw a Mexican mother with a child at the balcony of our house. But even though they were very friendly to me, they didn't enter the house. This was opposite of the Mexican cultural ethos which maintains that: "my house is your house." When I was ministering the Mexican, they never expected me to call them before the visit. When, I was seeking to know the meaning of the dream, I realized that the vision was reminding me that I need to put more effort in reaching out to the Mexican.

To my greatest surprise, the following day I found a Mexican lady at the clinic who spoke fluent Swahili. She had gone for mission in Tanzania where she learned Swahili.

When your babe see you shaking hand and being friendly to all races, you are training your child to interact with all human races.

You are equipping him to draw from and to impart to all races and to brake cultural barriers. You are connecting him/her to the multitude universal humanity.

Another surprising episode took plan at Chicago airport as my wife and I was waiting to board to plane to Boston. The mother was hold her baby who cried with allowed voice. Instead of spanking the baby the mother held the baby and put him in her breast and sooth him tenderly. Eventually the baby was quiet. As I was being impressed by the way the mother was handling the baby, a voice whispered to me: "that child will be a great man of God." The mother and the baby interred the plane before us. When we boarded the plane, as we were passing, the baby grumbled my thump tightly and gave me a wins one smile. Using nonvable language the baby was saying: "I will not let you go until you bless me." And so, I laid my hand on him and told him: "You will be a bishop." It is amazing how the Holy Spirit uses nonviable communication in impartation. Remember what He said to Jeremiah: "before I form you in the womb, I knew you, before you were born, I set you apart, I appointed you as a prophet to the nations." Jeremiah 1:5

The Fruitful Family

A nine months Mohamed became my hero as we were flying from Nairobi to Frankford. I had sat with his father who was speaking loudly and laughing with other Arab men. He avoided eye contact with me. As he was throwing his hand making me uncomfortable, I shouted: "Sir!" When he learned that I was black American he started gossiping the American with other Arabs who were several rolls away from us.

Six hour later little Mohamed was brought to the father by the mother.

When the little angel was brought by the mother, he grumbled my fourth finger and gave me a winsome smile. He held my fourth finger for a long time even though the father didn't gave me eye contact. He has learned from his friendly mother that he can reach out to all human being-black, white, red and yellow. In contrast, I went to West Gate mall, Amarillo at children play ground. I sat next to a Mexican mother. I greeted her but she didn't respond or even look at me. Her Four-year daughter who was playing with other children ran to the mother complaining that another child has stepped on her and didn't' say sorry. I tried to reach out to the child to console her. But the little girl didn't even look at me. Being the father of many nations, I remember a critical episode with my Mexican parishioners. When I visited them, I found children in tear. The husband who was undocumented and was having problem getting job said: "Father John, I have to be strong for my family. My wife spent long hour with a dentist. She came home with lot of pain. Before entering the house, she was arrested and now she in a cell and I don't have money to bill her out." As he shared this story, his two children were crying over my shoulders. After consoling them I gave them the money for billing their mother out.

Another excited episode took place at Retina clinic where I was undergoing racer surgery. As we were living, I saw two years old girl with her grandpa. The little angel looked at me fondly and then waive me goodbye. Even thou she was white she was saying to me: "May God be with you. You are also my grandpa."

Dr. John Githiga

As I was interacting with international children and parents, I had a dream in which I saw a Mexican mother with a child at the balcony of our house. But even though they were very friendly to me, they didn't enter the house. This was opposite of the Mexican cultural ethos which maintains that: "my house is your house." When I was ministering the Mexican, they never expected me to call them before the visit. When, I was seeking to know the meaning of the dream, I realized that the vision was reminding me that I need to put more effort in reaching out to the Mexican.

To my greatest surprise, the following day I found a Mexican lady at the clinic who spoke fluent Swahili. She had gone for mission in Tanzania where she learned Swahili.

When your babe see you shaking hand and being friendly to all races, you are training your child to interact with all human races.

You are equipping him to draw from and to impart to all races and to brake cultural barriers. You are connecting him/her to the multitude universal humanity

As I continued contemplating at Jesus statement: "Let the little children come to me continued waiving them and they remarkable responded. I started seeing the face of Christ in them. Surprising they started fronteering to waive. On one day I was walking in the West Gate Mall which was congested. A three old girl who was walking with her mom looked at me and waived. I waived back and told the mother: "this child is very friendly." She never see a stranger." Responded the great mother. Another day Mary were seating at Westgate more. A white mother was walking with her two and half year old. The little angel who was having a hand bag with her right hard waived with her left hand. The mother took the bag and brought her to us and asked her to shake our hands. The shopkeeper who was watching the drummer, came to us and said: "That is a good mother. She is leading that child to right path." This is indeed the right path for she was leading her girl to break cultural barriers and thus become cosmopolitan who will have ability to impart and draw from other communities. She was

The Fruitful Family

indeed training her to become a part of all Saints–who come from all nations, tribes and a language.

Another startling experience occurred at Walmart pharmacy. I was on line and a Mexica mother talking with Pharmacist while his three years old son was standing on a shopping cart. He was hipper and as he was jumping in the cart he was about to fall and I grumble him before he fell. The divine within revealed to the boy that I am a hand shake. The boy called his dad who was seral yard away. He called his dad loudly and persistently: "Dad! Dad! Dad!" reluctantly the father came and the little angel asked him to shake my hand. As we were shaking hands the father told me that he was moving slowly because he was too old: "How old are you?" I asked. "I am fifty yours old." "I am 26 years your senior." As we were hold dialogue Oma was jubilant because not only, we had hand shake and we were holding dialogue. This shows that God can use children to break cultural burrier.

Another uplifting episode occurred on Christmas at a Sudanese Church.

This was preceded by celebration of our Golden wedding anniversary on December 15, 2018. The event was a climax of supernatural tsunami of grace which we experience in 2018. We were owed by the growth of the seed which we planted many years ago in Kenya and the appreciation we received from the people of God.

However, witnessing frenetic favor put us in receptive mode of human consciousness. Our loving Father didn't put us on the stage on Christmas. We don't even send Christmas cards. Rather, the Spirit took us a Sudanese church ministered by our students Rev Michel Getkak and Maburu Atak. There we were ministered by a 3 years girl who was clad in beautiful dress. She was walking graciously looking whether there was someone who needed something. Looking at us, she noted that we were not Sudanese. She went to the box which had Neur and Dinka hymnals. There she sported an English Bible and brought it to us. After the service, we were given lot of food to take with us. We were both Spiritually and physically nourished.

The point here is that God, can use children to feed us. Remember Jesus used a boy's lunch to feed five thousand men. It is by receiving from the people of God, including children that we can become fruitful.

CHAPTER 3

AUTONOMY 3-6 YEARS

According to Erik Erikson the basic issue with a child is autonomy. The favorite word is "no" They like the word: No!" They need protection but not overcontrol. The parents and parent figure are representative of God. They learn that God is strong or weak, he is forgiving or unforgiving; he is helpful or worthless. What is at stake is the parent's reaction of their urine and feces. If they are punished for this, they develop a defense mechanism know as projection and introjection. As adults they project the evil within to others and in introjection, they will pay more attention to the evil around them. For example, these individual, when they enter your house, they will pay more attention to your garbage container than the clean part of the house. They are more concern with your weakness than your strength. They are habitual slanderers.

Theologically, at this age they perceive God as either good or evil; forgiving or unforgiving; helpful or worthless, Mary and

Dr. John Githiga

I spent several days with brother Gideon and Habel They both had three years old grandchildren who behaved differently. But they both claimed their autony. GG is a boy and whenever he comes in, he will give us five. If he does not fill slit pain, he said: haijaingia (it is incomplete). So, he will repeat and when you fill a little pain, he will say: "it is complete." One day he was stacking five chairs together, and when he was unsuccessful because he was too short for the task, his grandma tried to help. He cried because he wanted to do it alone. Here he was training himself to do his best independently.

Three and half year old, Mercy, who addressed Mary and I as grandpa and grandma of America had undertaken to be our tour guide, hostess, a carpenter and executive Director. To our surprise, we were led to Habel's home by Mercy. It was late in the evening. As we were just about to pass the path to my brother's home. Mercy, shouted to us: "where are you going?" we then realized that we were going astray and then followed our guide. Mercy's chore, included clearing the table after meal. If she saw a sport, she spate on it and wipe it with a napkin.

One day she had a surprise for her American grandparents. "I have money for you." She said this while she was unzipping the inner pocket of her jacket. She then gave each one of us two tea leaves. We received the money with great appreciation. The other amusing episode was when Mercy was doing construction with her grandpa. We were surprised seeing her cutting a piece of wood just like her grandpa who is a carpenter. When the grandpa took the saw to cut the same wood putting it on a chair. He was given a strong warning. "If you cut the chair, I will beat you and grandma and kick you out of the house, and I will stay with grandpa and grandma of America." In this regard she was behaving like Executive Director. The gracious grandpa was not offended.

When they are learning their role the parents and the those who take care of them should not expect them to be perfect. They will improve in the course of time. At the meantime, the child is learning from the loving adults around them. Interestingly, as I was

The Fruitful Family

writing this page, I gave Mercy's father a call to congratulate him for the newly born baby: "congratulation for a baby boy." "Don't call him a baby." He responded, "He is a Preacher! He is on his way to the pulpit." This is because he is Habel, Stephone's Father, who is a Preacher. So, Like Mercy, he is given a name which defines his role. Hence the very name mercy motivated the three years old to be philanthropologist. So, she strongly feel that she should give her American grandparents money.

I was surprise to see two years old Meru boy named Elijah Mothomi. According to the Meru costom, grandfather is consulted during the naming rite. The father had decided to call the boy Elijah, but the father recommended Mothomi which means a Student. Subsequently the child was give the two names. To the surprise of the parents, Muthoni became interested in books since year one. In his second year he was reading and able spell English words. He was asked to spell the word helicopter, to our greatest surprised the boy spelt the word correctly.

So, to be a fruitful family, the child should be trained for work, at the earliest age. When training they should not be expected to do it as an adult.

The parents of three and half years old were surprised to hear a sound of a vacuum cleaner. Looking, they saw the little girl vacuuming. When they asked her how and why she is doing it. She said: "I am vacuuming the devil for making me sin against my parents." This girl was training to be a preacher who will fight a good fight of faith.

The above child had similar attitude with a three years girl whom I met with her gland mother at a dollar Store. I waved to her but she didn't respond. I then told her grandmother that; "This child will be a good student." "She is very smart." Responded the grandmother.

CHAPTER 4

INDUSTRY AND WORK 7-12 YEARS

At this stage the main lesson to be learned is industry and work. They have to be guided to balance between work and play. If they are not trained at this age, they become useless and eventually they will be engages in fruitless life of taking drug and juvenile delinquency has also be remembered that work, work without play make Jack a dull boy. In our family of origin, at this age were fully engaged in school and work. I was both a herd boy and a farm. This occupation prepared me to the ministry. I learned how to deal with fighting cow, lamb and donkey. At the age of seven year I didn't know how to keep as safe distance from a donkey. On one occasion, I was too close to a donkey which give me a big kick with both legs, I flew in the air, and saw the stars and was unconscious for a long time. This trained me to keep a safe distance from a fighting parishioner. I also learned farming. How to prepare the seed bed and wait for germination, growth and harvest. I was surprised to learn that the seed of a plant which has the longest life took longer time to germinate. The bean would germinate within a week while a tea plant would take three weeks. This plant can live for two

The Fruitful Family

hundred and fifty years. This has been true to planting the seed for kingdom of God.

To prepare a fruitful family, the training for work must start very early. As the Bible puts it "Train the child the way he will follow and he will not depart from it." The Bible also make is clear that "He who does not work, let him not eat.

The Bible also exhort us: "by love, serve one another." We have to train children at this age to serve our neighbor. Mary and I are surprised by our neighbor, Josh, police offer, who has trained his 9 years old son to mow our yard. Surprisingly, this boy would not accept money. Kevin has seen the love which his parents have for us. Josh has rendered sacrificial service to the only black family in the neighbor. At one time we had a broken gate. We were so surprise by when and the way worked on the gate. On the material day, it rained from morning to evening that Mary and I don't get out of the house. Josh was also moving to another state the following day. Surprisingly, when we got out, we found the new gate and the Angel has moved to another state. This is indeed an amazing love. This is an example to show that a fruitful neighbor serves their neighbor by love.

CHAPTER 5

SELF IDENTITY 13-20 YEARS

The issue at this age is self-identity or role confusion. To be or not to be is the question This is the age of Initiation, confirmation, bar mitzvah. Pear group is extremely importance which replace parents and authority figures. Dependence or independent—dependent on alcohol and drug or God. This is the age of puberty which is often, but not always stormy. At this age they are bothered by increase of wait or Hight. There is great intake of food. They are bothered by being over wait or under wait; being too short or too tall. They are also bothered by motor awkwardness; the growth of primary and secondary sex organs; unevenness of sexual maturation. In this age they are influence by media.

PASTORAL ACTION

AT THIS AGE THE MOST important doctrine is humanity. Thus, the teens ask with the Psalmist: What is man that thou art mindful of him. The son of man that you care for him." Interestingly during a confirmation service one teenage come up with two

The Fruitful Family

titles: Christian. I am fearfully and wonderfully made. Since they are Christians and fearfully and wonderfully made. They need to learn that the body is the temple of the Holy Spirit. And thus, they need to be filled by the Holy Spirit. My brother Habel and I chose this path. Filled by the Holy Spirit we preached the Gospel everywhere in Nakuru, Kenya. We preached to Africans, Asians and European. On one occasion my brother was cursed by an Indian: He responded: "Thank you so much. You have revealed that you are sick and lost in sin and this is why I am preaching to you." On one episode, I stopped a European who shouted to me: "No!" "Jesus is willing to save you." Do you understand the meaning of the word no? I am going to put you in prison? To this I responded: "First will be last: and the last will be first." These words were put in my mouth by the Holy Spirit. And it is more than likely that this man committed himself to Christ.

Surprisingly we became so famous and feared–The Roman Catholic Church waned the members of the religion of a young man known as Gatungu. So, whenever we visited catholic family– They would quickly say: "we are Catholic." The image I had for myself is that of being connected to Universal power. Interestingly, when Mary and I were working at St. Nicholas's children home which we founded. We were visited by a lady who was full of joy. The lady asked me: "Can you remember something you did fifteen years ago? "No." I responded. Let me telling what you did. You came and found three women. One of them was working on the hair of one of the ladies. So, you came and told us "there is something which is more important that hair. Jesus Christ." When you said that I cursed you. After cursing you my hand was dislocated and had lot of pain and could not work hair any more. I then went home and told my daughter about a crack young man. My daughter told me 'mom you committed a great sin. That young man is a man of God and he is the one who teaches us religion.' When my daughter said that I had pain in my chest and in the midnight, I committed myself to Christ. Then I decided that I will be as that you man. I became a street preacher. And one man whom I won to Christ became a preacher. And he has won more than eight hundred people to Christ." This story tell us that if we equip teens for ministry. They will do great things for God.

At this age the church need to have program such as Boys and Girls Brigade. The moto of the Boys Brigade is : "Sure and steadfast." And the Girls Brigade motto is: "seek and follow Christ." Youth camps are very important, on addition to nurturing them in Christian faith, they need to learn about friendship between boys and girl and how remain faithful to God and to their future married partners.

In this age they can reach where the parents may not reach.

For example, I attended. attended First Christian Church where the teen, named Nicholas was passing the collection plate. It happened to be the only black person and the only person who put a check in the plate. Nicholas pet me on the back with his tender hands and said: "Thank you so much for the offering." It so happened that I have never had that experience in my life. Thus, if we quip children and youth to plant the seed of the Gospel the church will have a church is preaching from everywhere to everybody.

In USA where it is illegal teacher and adults to preach in schools, Teens will do this successfully.

CHAPTER 6

YOUNG ADULTHOOD 21–39

At this stage they either attain intimacy or isolation., with either constructive or distractive behavior. They are either Spirit filled or alcoholic and drug addict. If they take drug and alcohol, the become extremely dangerous to their parents and spouses. I know of the parent who have moved and would not let their drug addict son know where they are.

However, there are great programs for helping those who has gone astray. These include Alcoholic Anonymous and Teen and Adult Challenge. I know of a good number of individuals who have be helped by these programs. As it is in the earlier stages, Christ is the answer. When they commit themselves to Christ, the Holy Spirit will lead them from within and they will bear much fruits. They plant the right seeds in their families and to the members of the church. This is the best age to do children ministry. To train as Officers of Boys and Girls brigade and youth leaders.

It was at this age that I was trained as Church Captain. The motto of the society is: "fight a good fight." We were trained on evangelism and urban mission. We were equipped to reach where a priest may not reach. And the bishop gave me the ministry of reaching out to juvenile delinquents and eventually we established St. Nicholas's children home. Which birthed two other homes which bear the same name. In April last year (2018) we attended special thanksgiving service in Nairobi Cathedral which was attended by over 2000. Among the choirs which sang was St. Nicholas' Nairobi. The song that they was PLANT THE SEEDS. Mary and I were thrilled by remember that this home was born by the one we planted in Nakuru. Thus, my reader, I am encouraging plant the seed.

When Mary and I were ministering the troubled children at St. Nicholas's. We ere trained by Rev Ian Peterson, a Presbyterian Scottish Minister as officer of Boys and the Girls Brigade. And we started the very first Brigade company in Kenya. I became the first captain of the company and today there are companies all over Kenya in Anglican, Methodist and Presbyterian Churches. Joyfully, the Lord allows us to eat the fruits of our labor. During our honey moon, Rev Ian hosted us in his mansion, living us with his cook who provided us with meal include bred room coffee.

CHAPTER 7

GENERATIVITY AND CREATION 40-55 YEARS

If the person has been fruitful in the previous stages. The main focus at 40–55 years is generativity and creation. The energy is directed toward guiding the next generation. The major question is: "If I am only for myself, what am I? If not now when? this calls for courage of moving from known to unknown. You continue being a man/woman of vision. As with previous states and our work with God, we learn that God does not give vision without provision, but there is always a problem between the vision and provision.

It was at age, after spending elven years in theological institutions and attaining five theological degrees, that I became a Tutor at St. Paul United Theo local College. Became the head of Pastoral theology department. I taught a course entitled Human Background to Pastoral Ministry which had four units–Sociology, Sociology of Religion, Psychology, Psychology of Religion. The challenge I had was that there were no books in this field which were written by African. The student boycotted the class demanding that I recommend books which are authored by Africans. I took this as a call to research and write theological books.

Dr. John Githiga

Additionally, I was Director of Field Education and the Dean of Anglican Students. Being one of the few African Tutors with automobile, my car was paramedic and the student would awake me at midnight to take them to the hospital I may be in the hospital until 3am and I had to be in the class at 8pm.

Denominationally, I was Provincial Correspondent of the then Church of the Province of Kenya. I had a blessing of representing the church to Afro Anglican conference which was held in Barbados. I led the service in one of the Anglican Church in Barbados. What surprised me when I was shaking hands with congregant was a member who asked me: Father John, can you speak English?" Later, I share this question with a British man who told me that he was asked the same question to which he responded: "We manufactured the language." So, I learned that every community has its own fashion of English language just as it has its own cultural ethos.

The other most challenging undertaking was organization was of a conference of African pastoral counselling. I was given this assignment by Prof Masamba ma Mpolo of World Council of Churches. The conference which brought together Pastoral counselling from all over the world congregated in Limuru Conference Center, Kenya. I was a solo local organizer. During the conference it was resolved that we had to form African Association for Pastoral Counseling. I was unanimously elected its first President. After the departure of the new organization, I was left alone, with no funding to run the organization. Communication within African continent was tougher than overseas. I however succeeded communicating with three African professors who were the office bearers Through God's provision, we were invited by A German Professor who had attended the conference. She informed me that German Government would provide travelling expenses if I can write a letter to proof that African Association will be beneficial too German government. I don't remember what I wrote, but the Germans gave us fund for out traveling expenses to attend German Association for pastoral counselors.

The Fruitful Family

While we were there we work on the constitution for the African Association and planned to hold Congress on African Pastoral Counselling which had to take place in Kinshasa, Democratic Republic of Congo in summer of 1988. We enjoy our time in Germany which included sightseeing. By the time we hand to attend the Congress, I had already moved to the United States. So, I took with me two African American women delegates from Pensacola Florida. Prof Mengi, who came for us at the airport drove decisively and aggressively. One of the Ladies shouted to him: "slow down." To this Dr Mengi who is not accustomed being commanded by a woman responded with broken English. "Me, Dr Mengi driving!" The lady shouted: "we do not want to die:" our host shouted: Me, Doctor, Professor Bishop driving. Die go to heaven." So, the driver took us to Kibangu conference center and put the ladies in one room with one bed. The ladies besought Professor to take them where they would stay in a Motel. But the professor, knowing that that was the best motel, left the ladies and disappeared. The challenge which I faced as the President was that I was expected to address the Congress in French. Here, the climate of the public opinion was that every educated person must be able to speak in French. However, I succeeded in getting un interpreter. It however appeared to my Congolese colleague that I was too democratic. So, they warned me that democracy will not work: "you must dictate!" It was tough for me to dictate but I had no choice. Among the things that I dictated is that I have to hand over my position to Masamba Ma Mpolo. And this was unanimously agreed. Beside attending the Congress, we had time for site=seeing. In deed enjoyed my time in Congo. And I most grateful to my laving Father for giving me this assignment and for using me to the maximum.

CHAPTER 8

OLD AGE

Traditionally the Kikuyu had a rite of passage known as Ituika which means land. It was time to landslide to Menengai which was the place of the living dead. It was believed that if you go to this place, you will see he living dead gracing their animals; but if you approach them, they will vanish. The living dead they were visible but not touchable. When my maternal Gatungu was in this stage, he used to tell me "Gatungu, I am waiting for my passport to go to Miningai.

Those who fail in the previous stages end up with disappear stagnation. The fear death because it will rob them the time try all over again. According to Erik Erikson those who have succeeded in previous stages attains integrate. They go back go basic trust.

At this age the main theological theme is euchology which is rather personal eschatology.

There is a gradual releasing of authority and power. It is a time for Preparation of the living will and the power of the attorney. The temptation of the member of the family is to abandon their loved one at this age. I use to visit a member of my church who was at this age who constantly complain that her only daughter has taken vacation from her. Another parishioner who was a retired profession and bipolar would give a condition to me when I was praying for her. "please don't pray that God keep me any longer. I need t go home." Also being bipolar, I could find her in her worst negative condition. For instance, I paid her a pastoral visit in the hospital. She shouted at me: "do not enter hear." "Why." I responded: "The virus I have is deadly." "Nolly, you are treating me like your student." I responded. "I am bacteriologist and I know the bacteria I have is deadly." And so, left her quietly. Two days later I called her care giver and asked: How is Nolly? "she Is as good as she can be." So, I visited her. Being legally blind, I was surprised by her comment as I was entering the house: "You look so tired>" and she was very right because I was actually tired. To my greatest surprise. her last week on earth, she was consistently good. So, the message is that we should be with our loved at this age whether they are mentally sick or depressed. This work can be done well by pastoral team. The same ministry is required for terminally sick.

More importantly, the member of the family should take care of the aging parent. The fourth commandment challenges us to "honor your father and mother so that all may well with you" As we shall see later, God and the parents are the filters through which we receive heavenly and earthly graces. Not only that we have their jeans and architypes, we have their names. We also have the name which were given to us when we were baptize. So, we now turn to this vital subject.

CHAPTER 9

THE EFFECT OF THE NAMES ON PERSONALITY

Interestingly I was given the title, Padre (Father) by my mother's mid-wife who was maternal grandmother. The formula which was used when I appeared was: "whom have you seen?" asked the father. The midwives responded: "we have seen men and it is your father in law." Name after her father, it was disrespect to her father to mention my name. When I was a toddler, I would cry and would not keep quiet until she soothed me with a magic word: "stop crying my dad.' She, however stopped this habit on a night when I cried for a long time waiting to hear the magic word. She put off the light and went to bed and left me in the dark. Scared of the darkness, I never cried again for the title. But the community picked a title for me. According to our culture, it is disrespect to call a mother by her name. So, the community gave her the name Wagatungu. Gatungu being the name of my grandpa. So Wagatungu has a double meaning: The daughter of Gatungu and the Mother of Gatungu.

Interestingly, the name I was given by my mother and our community became my title. In Canyon and Amarillo, Texas, I am

The Fruitful Family

referred as Father John, Padre John, Abuna (Arabic for father) in India they address me and Mary, Father and Mother and in one family they have two sons both of who are John. In Pakistan they like calling me Papa and in Embu, Dad and Babu (grandpa) and in ANCCI my official title is Patriarch, which means the father of many nations. Interestingly I was given the title by Mary long before we established ANCCI. She like using this title when she is calling me for dinner. She calls: "The father of human beings (*Ithe wa andu*) dinner is ready." I like calling her darling, the mother of human beings, my lover. After the celebration of our Golden wedding anniversary, she got a new title: "Golden Girl"

When we were preparing for mission to Kenya this year (2019), God used the names of our mothers for mission statement. Our both mother's baptism name is Joyce. Mother was given this name by a missionary who asked her about the name she would like. "I am a joyous person and therefore I would like the name which defines my character. She was then given the name Joyce. When we were praying for mission at St. Cyprian International church. Rev Sue Sanborn told us to enjoy our mission. So, we came up with the a mission statement: **enjoy.** Our first this which we have to enjoy was a tough question we were asked by the security officers at Houghton as we were preparing to board the plane. They were having a dog which smelt money in us. The officer pulled us aside and asked: "Tell us about all the money which both of you have. Mary quickly said: "we put our money in the bank." I then joyfully took the wallet out of my pocket and opened the wallet and showed the officer all the money that I had in the wallet. After looking the wallet, he said: "just go." Thus, the joy of the Lord became our strength.

The lesson here is that the name we give to our children has some effect on their personality and profession and ministry.

Remarkably the prayer of the parents of the great men of God, like Samuel and John the Baptist defined their children mission. For Hanna, her Son whom she dedicated to God after weaning, he will minister to the Lord with the joy of the Lord and will bring victory to Israel and will proclaim the holiness of God. His ministry will brought cultural transformation in that "those who were hungry hunger no more. "The Lord sends poverty and wealth; he humbles and exalt. He raises the poor from the dust and lift the needy from the ash heap; he set them with princes and has them inherit a throne of honor" (see Samuel 2:1–10) As Hanna predicted, her son became a powerful prophet, priest and a Judge. And by donating and dedicating him to God, she was given seven children.

Excitingly, Zachariah's song (Luke 1:68–79) predicts the mission of his son. Luke reports that Zachariah "was filled by the Holy Spirit and prophesied." John will preach about redemption, repentance, restoration and will preach without fear and will prepare the way for the Messiah. John really possessed the quality of the true prophet. He was humble before God and bold before men. He referred to himself as: "A voice of one calling in the desert, Prepare the way of the Lord, make straight for him. Every valley shall be filled in, every hill made low. The crooked road shall become straight, the rough ways smooth. And all mankind will see God's salvation." Luke 3:4–6. Here John is declaring his mission statement which include, cultural, economic and spiritual transformation. John was so bold that he could welcome the new commers with this word: "You brood of vipers! Who warned you to flee from the coming wroth? Produce fruits in keeping with repentance. Do not begin to say to your selves: 'we have Abraham as our father.' For a telling you that out of these stones God can raise up children for Abraham." Luke 3:7–8 Finally, the Baptist was killed for the prophetic message to the king whom he challenged for marrying his brother's wife.

When my father chose the name John for me, did he had John the beloved disciple or the Baptist in mind? Being a teacher, preacher and prophet, he had both in mind. In my long ministry I have a blessing of being Jeremiad both in Kenya and United states. The church which called me to the USA fired me for being faithful to whom who said: "Be faithful to death and I will give me the crown of life."

The Fruitful Family

The following pages epitomizes What I went through after doing fruitful and prophetic ministry in Pensacola Florida and how the saint stood with me.

While we enjoyed a fruitful ministry and the love of the people of God in Pensacola Florida, the devil was plotting against us. He used the same method as he used with Joseph. The Bible tells us that God blessed Potiphar because of Joseph, his slave. His success attracted Potiphar's wife and she asked Joseph, "Come to bed with me." When he refused, she had him put to prison? Genesis 39:1–23. In my case the Potiphar's wife tried to seduce me several times, but when she found that I was not yielding, she said, "I will put you on the street." I didn't understand what she meant by putting me on the street.

About this time the first edition of "*Christ and Roots*" had been published. This coincided with a Diocesan Clergy Conference. So, joyfully and naively I presented the book to the Bishop and asked him to mention the book to the Clergy. His face turned red and he remarked, "So you spend all your time writing books instead of ministering the parish?" From that time, he was looking for ways to get rid of me. This incident was followed by an Episcopal visitation. The seductive woman had an audience with the Bishop. She accused me of AFRICAN-NESS AND ACCENT. The following day she gave me a call and said, "Father, forgive me for lying to the Bishop about you." I asked, "Could you pick up the same phone and tell the Bishop that you lied to him?" She retorted, "Sorry, I don't have the courage to do so." The following day I found she had left a present for me in the office.

After this incident, I was invited by the Bishop to his office. I took my wife with me. The Bishop quickly came to the point. With a heavy southern accent, he said, You have to go because of two things, "AFRICAN-NESS AND ACCENT."

After the judgment Mary held the Bishop by the shoulders and said, "Bishop, let me ask you a question." "Yes, Mary," responded the Bishop. "Are you a Christian?" "Yes, I am" said the Bishop." "If you are a Christian, be listening to good people and not to bad people. It can be cold there. Be a shepherd to your priests." On this note we left the Bishop and we never saw him again.

After this, one of the Wise Virgins,[1] who was a Professor, visited with the Bishop and asked him why he had fired their priest. "It is not me, it is the Church Council," he claimed. Then she confronted the Church Council and they said, "It is not us; it is bishop."

What amazes me is that even though we were misjudged, we were not angry with the Bishop or the Church. We had a clear conscious for having done what the Lord wanted us to do. We felt fulfilled for the way God used the gifts which he had given us. And, indeed, we gave only what we have received from God and the church.

As Jesus asked the disciples : "Who do people say that I am?" When they said: "some say you are Elijah, or John the Baptist or one of the Prophet. He then asked them: "And whom do you say that I am." And so, I asked the members who have been with me for five fruitful years to write their testimonial about me. So, as the following testimonies from the Senior Warden and Altar Director indicates, we developed the congregation by starting and empowering several programs: Youth programs, Women of the Church, Men's fellowship, Bible studies which met in the Church and homes. We connected the church to spiritual movements such as Kairos and Cursillo. Mary and I, having been brought up in an ecumenical city, Nakuru, Kenya, were ministers of all people of God in Pensacola, Florida

---

[1] The Parable of the Ten Virgins, also known as the Parable of the Wise and Foolish Virgins, is one of the parables of Jesus. According to the Gospel of Matthew 25:1–13, the five virgins who are prepared for the bridegroom's arrival are rewarded, while the five who are not prepared are disowned. The parable has a clear theme: be prepared for the Day of Judgment. John Barton, The Oxford Bible Commentary, Oxford University Press, 2001.

The Fruitful Family

We did the following:

MOTIVATIONS PROGRAMS FOR COLLEGE BOUND

We invited African and African-American Professors from University of West Florida and Pensacola Junior College to motivate the community. They all made great presentation on the importance of education. Consequently, a good number of participants enrolled in the College and the University. Consequently, I was invited to motivate students in middle schools and high schools.

DIALOGUE BETWEEN POLICE OFFICERS AND THE COMMUNITY.

In those days Pensacola ranked number six in crime in Florida. We were led by the Spirit to bring together law enforcement officers and citizens. We even invited the criminals. But humorously, instead of attending the dialogue, they stuck their hair in the door to the parish hall where the meeting was taking place. Many useful questions were raised, such as, "Someone is breaking in the door, and when I call 911, you have to keep on asking questions instead of coming at once. Why do you do this?" A Police Officer answered, "When you call, we start driving to your home immediately, but we keep you on the phone so as to know what is going on." At the end of the session, there was a better understanding between the Officers and the community.

WE ALSO TAUGHT IN PENSACOLA JUNIOR COLLEGE

in the Department of Humanities. Courses included; Humanity in the ancient World, Humanity in modern World, Humanity and Art. I had two classes. One of the classes had civilian students. The other was for military students at the Naval and Air Bases. I was surprised to note that the military students did better than the civilians. They were also more adventurous. For instance, in a class on Humanity and Art, they asked me whether they could visit our home for dinner so that they might see African Arts in food. I told them that I have to ask my wife because that is her department. Reporting to Mary, she told me that she would also like to see the American art in cooking. So, we decided to have a covered dish featuring American and African foods. To motivate my daughter to join the Navy, I asked that a few of them come in Navy Uniforms. We enjoyed cerebrating with African and American food. Hence forth, our daughter's greatest desire was to join the Navy. She did this after graduating from High School.

BREAKING CULTURAL BARRIERS was another ministry that the Creator entrusted to us. In my office we had weekly fellowship with two Anglo priests. Most of the time we were so surprised to note we had related blessings and challenges. On one occasion, the Loving Father accorded me a humorous episode. A white priest who was going on vacation asked me to supply for him. In his church there was a parishioner who have vowed that he could not take communion from a black priest. However, the church was well attended. After service the generous church members took me out for lunch. This new friend happened to sit next to me at the table. Then in the group a humorous man reveals the secret to me, "Father, the man sitting next to you had said that he cannot take communion from a black Priest, we were so surprised that he took communion from you." "I particularly came because of him," I responded. He responded: "When I saw you, I said, 'ministerial Alliance' is here. But when you preached, I had a different view. I said to myself, I wish our priest could stay away longer so that we can have more of you." I hugged the man and since then he became a new creation.

HEALING was another ministry that the Great Physician did through us. We had two girls who were afraid of water. Deed was eleven years old and was in baptism class. She was better than other children in memorizing The Apostles' Creed, the Ten Commandments and Bible verses. But any time we had a baptism, she could not come to Church. I asked her mother what she does when she needed a shower. "It is always a battle," said the mother.

The Fruitful Family

Mary and I visited the family at their home. I asked Deed to sit with me. I asked her, "Do you believe in God the Father, God the son and God the Holy Spirit?" "I do, she responded." "Do you want to be baptized in the name of the Father and the Son and the Holy Spirit?" "I do." "With warm or cold water?" "It does not matter." I then asked for water and baptized the girl. Tears were rolling down her cheeks. A few days later I received a card stating: "Thank you, Father Githiga, for baptizing me." I have baptized thousands of Christians, but she was the only person who has written a Thank-You card.

The other miracle was a ministry to 13-year-old Tomika. I noted her hydrophobia when we were crossing the bridge to Pensacola Beach, which is three miles long. Approaching the bridge, Tomika shouted: "Water!" and started shivering. So, on Sunday after church we took her and other youth to our home. I then asked her to come with me to the kitchen sink. I opened the faucet and told her, "This is the same as the water at the beach. It is harmless. I will pour some water on your hands and I want you to trust that it is not going to hurt you." So, I poured the water and I could see God healing the girl. After this we took her and other youth to the Beach. To our great surprise, Tomika was first to dash to the water. Her fear of water vanished completely.

God did many other great works through us, but we have shared these so as to encourage the many servants of God who have been betrayed, so they may know that they are not alone. And God will bless the seed that they have planted, and there are faithful people of God who see and appreciate your ministry. Better still, if you are being betrayed and finally thrown from the pulpit, do not curse the church. Bless the church! This is what we did in our farewell message.

DR. GITHIGA'S FAREWELL MESSAGE

As I look toward our departure, which is at hand, I express my gratitude to Almighty God, who called us to come and minister

Dr. John Githiga

at St. Cyprian's Church in Pensacola, Florida. The Supreme Being had planned our being together before the foundation of the world. I greatly praise the Giver of all things for the way He has used the gifts which He has given me and my family. I am grateful to my family who have willingly ministered with me.

Mary has transported the members who had no transportation. She has sung in the choir, worked with Altar Guild, and youth, strengthened spirit of the men of the church and reminded me about small details such as putting the hymn numbers on the board and the prayers for the Birthdays.

Rehema has participated in Junior Chair and youth program; she calls young people on Tuesdays, reminding them of the choir practice and youth program. She started Nursery for babies.

Isaac Cyprian has attracted more babies to St. Cyprian's. He has, however, the propensity of attracting more girls than boys.

My tremendous appreciation goes to the Church of God at St. Cyprian's Church. These faithful Christians, ecclesia in ecclesia, have given us moral support, useful advice and encouragement. They have indeed been pastors to us. We have always felt loved and taken care of. I have never felt discriminated against by the Church in the Church on the basis of my personality type or nationality or accent. This church, being the creation of the Holy Spirit, has discerned, cherished, used our gifts of the Spirit. She has indeed appreciated our gifts and drawn from the wealth of our spirituality. I will ever be grateful to the Church which has boldly enthroned Christ.

It is my prayer that God will continue to sustain, guide, illumine and keep his church after our departure. Our separation is temporary since at the end of all things, we will dwell in our Father's house forever. Since my contract expires on August 31, I will take my annual leave on August 1. My family will be leaving toward the end of August. If I don't have a job in this country, I will depart a few months after August.

May the peace of God be with you and remain with you always.
The Rev. Dr. John G. Githiga, May 12, 1991.

The Fruitful Family

The following testimonials highlight how we were perceived by the Church in Pensacola, Florida and by Bishop George Njuguna who was our Bishop before we left for United States:

RECOMMENDATION FROM ALTAR DIRECTOR:

TO WHOM IT MAY CONCERN

My name is Helen Edwards. I have been a member of St. Cyprian's Episcopal Church for thirty-five years. I am writing this letter on behalf of the Rev. Dr John Githiga who has served as our Vicar for five years. During his tenure at St. Cyprian's, I have observed many positive changes: such as the reactivation of men's club and Episcopal Church women organization, and increase in Sunday and mid-week church attendance, an increase in member participation in Diocesan activities at Camp Beckwith and summer camp for youth and the establishment of an Altar Guild and children's choir. Rev Githiga has been responsible for organizing weekly Bible Study and Prayer groups. He has encouraged church to attend Cursillo activities and other Diocesan workshops and seminars. I strongly feel that Rev. Githiga's sermons exemplify his profound ability to preach and teach. Also, he routinely ministers to the sick and shut-ins. As Altar Guide Directress, I have had the privilege of working closely with Rev Githiga. He has exhibited an even-temper which has been very necessary, as he worked with the diverse groups of communicants at St. Cyprian's Church. It is my pleasure to recommend the Rev. John G. Githiga as highly capable of fulfilling any position for which he may apply.

Sincerely,
Helen Edwards.

Dr. John Githiga

FROM THE SENOR WARDEN

JOSEPH F. YOUNG JR.
SENIOR WARDEN
July 14, 1991

TO WHOM IT MAY CONCERN:

It is my pleasure to submit this letter recommending the Rev. Dr John Githiga as a potential Rector of your parish. As a long time, communicant, Lay Reader, holder of various positions of responsibility and ultimately, Senior Warden in St. Cyprian's Episcopal Church, I have had opportunity to work and observe Dr. Githiga during the last five years. Dr. Githiga brought to this church a wealth of leadership qualities which proved to be beneficial to this congregation over the last five years.

In Church development, Dr. Githiga revived youth interest in the church through special youth programs including youth reading of the Lectionary on a regular basis on one Sunday of the month throughout each calendar year. Under his leadership, active membership attendance increased during the past five years. Lay participation in services increased proportionately. Through his guidance I have become more proficient in understanding and aiding in the administration of the Lay ministry as well as performing other duties assigned to me during his tenure. I am sure that I speak fora majority of this church when I say that we regret the financial situation1 at this time prohibits our retaining Dr Githiga as Vicar, and wish him success in being situated elsewhere in a deserving role of employment.

Sincerely,
Joseph F Young, Jr
Senior Warden

The Fruitful Family

Financial problems were a rationalization from the Diocesan office. After five years the church has grown in membership, participation, mission and stewardship. We paid Diocesan apportionment on time and we also got our compensation on time. This is why the bishop told us, "You have to go because of your African-ness and accent.

FROM DOCTRAL STUDENT GRAMBLING STATE UNIVERSITY

P.O. Box 3296
Grambling State University
Grambling, LA 71245

TO WHOM IT MAY CONCERN:

Dear Sir, I find Dr. John Githiga to be a highly intelligent theologian! I am impressed by his keen insight and his ability to use God's word as a tool to solve the complex problems of modern society. Dr. Githiga adds an Afro-centric approach to the Scriptures. He accomplishes this without compromising God's love and concern for all mankind. Since I have been admitted to Doctoral Studies at Grambling, I have benefited from his counseling and ministerial services. Furthermore, Dr. Githiga allows his members to express their opinions without compromising church or spiritual doctrines. He reminds me of men like Elijah and Daniel in his prophetic ministry. I view Father Githiga as an asset to God, Church and humanity! Therefore, I am honored to recommend him for your services.

Respectfully,
Tommy Johnson

THE NAME JOHN MEANS GOD is gracious. As you can see from the above pages, we received grace after grace. We were affirmed by the people of God. All the events which were aiming to crush us, God was working behind the scene. Whatever we lost because of Gospel; we gained a hundred folds. The greatest gift which we received is the ability to get out of the box which regarded Episcopal church as the church. We were amazed by the way we were received by other church families included non-denominal. We were received by Charity Chapel which had men fellowship which I attended regular. The Spirit guided us to start Fellowship which embraces people of all races. And it was in our home that Kenya Christian Fellowship in America was birthed. We held communion which had grape juice for the church family which does not use wine. And wine for the churches which us wine. To our surprised the Christian whose denomination do not use wine, they all took wine. Thus, the suffering made us more fruitful and a part of the universal Church.

We are startled by the way God send his angels when we are being afflicted. For instant after our last firing by the same church for reaching out to the Sudanese and for having undesirable member of the family living with us in the Vicarage. We experienced God's frenetic grace from angels. One angel gave us $5000; another gave us $3000 and then the other gave us $2000. God don't allow us to be homeless. And within two years, we had five rental properties. And three years after this persecution, God gave us ministry which was registered in the State of Texas as All Nations Christian Church international on July 27, 2007 which is my birthday. More about this in MINISTRY TO ALL NATIONS.

If you were given a belittling name, be in Christ and bear fruits and then claim the titles related to your fruitful ministry. I was first named Bishop by the student at Nakuru Boys Club where I was taking painting and signwriting. I was among the first intake of the school. I observed that we didn't have religious education. So, I went to the Principle and asked him whether he would get us someone who would teach us Religion. "Can you do it." He asked. "I can try." I responded. He then gave me 15 minutes from Monday to Friday to teach all protestants students. Things went on so well. The following semester he gave me 30 minutes and then the third semester, I was given 50 minutes. I heavily relied on the Holy Spirit since I didn't have formal religious education. Before the class start,

The Fruitful Family

I would go Bathroom and prayed in Spirit so that he may speak to the students throw me.

After theological education I was given new titles–Captain, Deacon, Padre (the title which I was given by my mother), Then after going through tribulations I was given more titles-Chancellor. Archbishop, Patriarch, John VIII; which mean that in our Apostolic succession which goes all the way to St. Peter, I am 13th Patriarch who is name John. This means that I am a Father of All Nations Christian Church International which grew from Anglican Church Worldwide. ACW grew from African Orthodox church which was established by Joseph Rene Villette in January5, 1892. Rene was ministering with Episcopal Church. After being elected bishop he was rejected consecration because he was black. Patriarch Rene refused the Racist to dine his ministry. So, he went all the way to South Africa and the Patriarch of African Orthodox Church agreed to consecrated. He succeeded in having three bishops. who included Old Catholic, Anglican and orthodox who consecrated him? And so, we have Apostolic succession from three main streams of Christendom. But what make us most grateful is Christ in us the hope of glory. And this is why our mission statement is: EMPOWERED BY THE HOLY SPIRIT, WE PREACH THE GOSPEL TO ALL NATIONS.

If you are in Christ, you are co-heir with Christ and for that reason you can claim all titles of the children of God. fill your lamp with oil a claim Christian heritage. You are a child of the King of Kings, a child of light. Vindicated, saved, God's delight. Isaiah 62:1–5.

A story is told of a teenager known as Patre Penda. He was visiting his sister and when he a lighted the bus, he saw a Police location with 52 homes. He was commanded by the Holy Spirit to visit each and every home.

When he was coming out of the last home a Police officer asked him: "who are you and who give you permission to enter Police homes." He responded: "I am a son of the King of Kings and I was commanded by the King to do so." "Get away from hear!" shouted the officer. And the teenagers filled with power and the joy of the Holy Spirit left the village.

The main point is that when you are belittled by the devil agents you need to allow the Spirit of Christ fill every fiber of your being and you will automatically bear the fruits of the Holy Spirit which is love, joy, pace, patience, kindness, goodness, faithfulness and gentleness and self–control. This is all what is need for a fruitful life. You need to bear in mind nobody has ever kicked a dead dog. Remember that while you have something superior you will have people who will feel jealousy. Remember the people who persecuted Jesus were those were the high priests, scribed and the Pharisees. They were jealousy of his mighty work. St. Thomas Aquinas, one of the greatest theologians, when he was at Cologne, was called by his classmates "the dumb Ox". To their surprise Thomas went on to receive a doctorate in the University of Paris, where he also taught. He eventually became one of the most respected Doctor of the Church.

Thus, if you were called diminishing name by your peer or the member of the family, look at yourself in the light of what the bible says about human being. Listen what the Bible says about you:

> What is man that that you are mindful of him?
> The son of man that you care for him?
> You have made him a little lower
> than the heavenly beings
> And crown him with glory and honor
> You have made him ruler of the work of your hands
> You put everything under his feet. Psalm 8:4–7

GIVE YOURSELF A BETTER NAME OR TITLE

REMEMBER WHEN THE PHARISEES REFERRED to Jesus as demon possessed, and a broker of Sabbath law; He referred to himself as the Lord of the Sabbath, the light of the world, the way, the truth, the life and resurrection.

The Fruitful Family

When the first president of Kenya, Jomo Kenyatta was accused of being a communist who was leading Kenya to darkness. He gave himself the two names. Jomo means a sword. Kenyatta while it means a belt decorated with beads, it also means the lamp of Kenya. After being imprisoned for eight years, when he was being released, he was interviewed by BBC. He was asked: "now that the British have imprison you for eight years, what are you going to do to the when you become a Prime Minister?" He replied: "We will forgive them and show them by our love that we a better than them." When he became Prime minister, he first met with his political activists who advised him that the settlers must be kicked out of the country immediately. But when he met with the settlers, he had a different message: "We have forgiven you and we also ask for your forgiveness. we are not going to confiscate your farms; but we are going to buy from you." He also organized that the European who were in leadership and had specialized job train the Kenyans before going home. The author has a blessing of undergoing through this process. He was trained by Rev John Ball, as Diocesan Youth organizer, the position which entailed training local youth leaders and Sunday school teachers and being the Secretary of Youth Department. The training included skill in office routine which helpful to him even today. Mary and I were trained by a Presbyterian Scottish missionary as officers of Boys and Girls Brigade which help us to start the firs company of the Boys and Girls Brigade which became the mother of Brigades companies in Kenya in Anglican, Methodist and Presbyterian churches.

So, Kenyatta vision allowed for successful transformation and this is why Kenya is one of the most developed countries in Africa.

In contrast, when Robert Mugambi of Zimbabwe became President, he kick out of the country all the settlers immediately. Consequently, Zimbabwe which was the shining star of Africa is now one of the poorest countries in Africa. Some years back we were in mission to Zambia. We visited Livingstone town. We crossed Zambezi River; I was surprised to buy 10 billing Zimbabwe dollars with $10. So, if you have $10, you are a billionaire by

Zambian standard. The country became so poor because of the name Mugambi gave to himself–Avenger and, unforgiving. So, to be fruitful, you have to forgive as Christ has advised us to forgive our enemies. In the family, many things will go wrong but we have to forgive each other. To error is human, to forgive is divine.

Thus, if you were given a demeaning name, give yourself a better name. better still, claim the titles which are found in the word of God which include; image of God, steward, blessed, fruitful, goodness (Genesis 1:26–:31), crowned with glory and honor (Psalm 8:5). If you are in Spirit, you are anointed preach the good news. The Bible says: You will be called a new name-righteousness, saved, Prince and princess, God's delight, bride, bridegroom. If you are in Spirit claim the names related to the fruit of Spirit: love, joy, peace, patience, kindness, goodness, faithfulness, gentleness, self-control. If you have these names you have character, and according to Booker T Washington Character is power. Character is also the bases of a fruitful family.

Hence, if you were given a condescending name, give yourself a better name. Better still, claim the titles which are found in the word of God which include; image of God, blessed, fruitful, goodness (Genesis 1:26–: 31), crowned with glory and honor (Psalm 8:5). If you are in Spirit, you are anointed to preach the good news. The Bible says: You will be called a new name-righteousness, saved, Prince and princess, God's delight, bride, bridegroom. If you are in Spirit claim the names related to the fruit of Spirit: love, joy, peace, patience, kindness, goodness, faithfulness, gentleness, self-control. If you have this name you have character, and according to Booker T Washington Character is power. Character is also the bases of a fruitful family.

CHAPTER 10

SEVEN FUNDAMENTALS FOR FRUITFUL FAMILY

1. Avoid alcohol and drugs and pornographic material. This are a deadly thing which would lead the family to destruction. Infortune, these are the deadly things which have affected a global village. Nearly each one of us know a family with drug and alcohol addiction person. In some cases, the situation is so bad that the parents have to flee from their sons or daughters with addition. The major problem is stealing money from the parents for buying drug. One of our friends with a son who is in drug has to flee from her son. She cannot even be in media because her son can google her and get the detail about her account. The parents who are having this problem need pastoral visits and the words of encouragement from the pastoral team.
2. *Avoid the company of the evil people.* The Bible tells us: "blessed is the man who does not walk in the counsel of the wicked or stand in the way of sinners or seats with company of mockers. But delight in the way of the Lord and on his

law he meditates day and night. The righteous replaces, evil thing with reading and meditating on the Law of the Lord. He is always in the company of the people who bear the fruits of the Holy Spirit. The righteous enjoy being in Bible fellowship, Sunday school, being in Boys and girls brigade, women of the church and men's fellowship. The reword of this relationship is great. Thus, in these productive groups are like trees planted by streams water, which yield its fruits in season and whose leaf does not wither and whatever they do prospers.". Being fruitful God watches over them. Psalm 1. These fruitful persons lift up their eye upon the hill from where they help come from. The loving Father who watches over them is the great Provider, Protector, Al powerful, all knowing and so in his hands they feel secure.

3. Do not provoke your children to anger. When you feel secure in the Lord and the love of God is flowing in your heart. You don't provoke your children to anger. When I was a 5th grader, I stayed with a family with a boy named Njuru (Nasty). I never saw the father having any friendly relationship with the boy. He used his leather belt to beat up the boy. The boy will run out and pick up rocks and threw them to the house without caring about whom he will hit. There are parents who have bad relationship with their children. Then the Children develop same attitude to the society and their parents as well. But we have to bring them up in discipline, and instruction and the love of the Lord. The blessing which we had in my family of origin, was that my dad had big dreams for us-Three things were most important to him: Church, school and work. The mother was a comedian. Joy and laughter was the most valued mode of life. She Taugher us human relationship. However, the most important thing is putting Christ at the center. This will lead to bearing much fruits.

The Fruitful Family

Children are exhorted: "obey your parents in the Lord for this is right. "honor you mother and father"–which is a first commandment with a promise–"that it may go well with you and that you may enjoy long life on earth. "I am a witness to this promise. My wife and I were obedient to our parents and consequently God has given use a healthy and fruitful life. At 77, I still have strength for writing, teaching, pastoral care. My motto is:

God, give me work,

Till my life shall end;

And life, till my work is done.

4. *Do not curse your children* You still need to keep on praying for your children even when they go astray. The shining example is Monica who's some Augustine was following the wrong company. Monica went to his bishop with tears. And the after bishop praying for the young man, he assured Monica: "it is not possible for a child of those tears get perish." After a while, Augustine heard a soft voice which led him to Christ. Subsequently, he became one of greatest doctors of the Church. It was from him that we leaned the meaning of "sacrament." He left to us one of greatest books entitled *CONFESSION*. Thus, even if your children deviate from the right path until your death bed. Bless them, they may because faithful servants of God after you are dead. And you will be surprised to be with them in heaven where you will rejoice with them forever.

5. *Respect and honor your spouse.* De realized that your spouse is the most important person to you and to your children. She is the very person to see when you wake up and the last person to see at night. Not only that he/she is with you most of time. And where you get sick, she is your first care giver. And according to Jesus Christ, you are one body. I

am so awed by Jesus understanding for the bode between a husband and a wife. Mary and I have been surprised by this mystery particularly when we have mis replaced something. For example, I will aske her: "Darling have you seen my glasses?" Before completing the sentence. Her senses are communicate to me. And then I have seen them. Thank you. The Bible advises us:' "Husband ought to love their wives as their own bodies. He who love his wife loves himself." Ephesian 6:28. Husbands we are advised: "Love your wives as just as Christ love the Church and gave himself up for her to make her holy." Ephesians 6:25. St. Paul give the best definition of the meaning of love. Listen. "Love is patient, love is kind, it does not envy, it does not boast, it is not proud, it is not rude, it is not self-seeking, it does not keep the record of wrong. Love does not rejoice with evil, but rejoices with truth. It always protect, always trust, always hopes, always persevere." 1Corinthian 13 4–This is indeed the best summary of the ingredients which are required for successful marriage and fruitful family. We automatically have this quality whenever we allowed the Hoy Spirit fill very fiber of our lives. I once asked married couple the secret of being able to stay in marriage for sixty year: the husband answered: "When we started the business, we asked Jesus to be the chairman of the board." Read more in the *Secret of Success in Marriage.*

6. *Balance between freedom and control.* Human life, like an automobile requires breaks and accelerator. In most cases one parents may be a break while the other is an accelerator. In the case of the Vitus the chromosomes of the father encourages growth, while the mother control. In our family I am the accelerator while Mary is the break. There is advantage and disadvantage on the both sides. At one time were shopping in the mall while our 5yeard Ray wanted to move about. I ask Mary to give her freedom to do so. Within a short time, the child disappeared. Searching for her, I

found she has gone outside the store and was heading to a busy highway. It is not always possible to balance between freedom and control. However, if the child is overcontrolled, he develop law self esteem and become less adventurous. If there is no control the child may become delinquent with inflated ego. The parents have to be patient with each other because breaks are as important as accelerator.

7. *Balance between work and rest* A fruitful family need to learn how to balance between work and rest. As it is said: "Work, with no play makes Jack a dull boy" On one hard the Bible says "He who does not work, let him not eat" Moreover the Bible says: "work out your salvation with fear and trembling." And then on the other hand: "For by grace are you saved through faith, not of work, rest anybody should boast." The family needs to have time to work together, but also time to have good time together–watching a movie together and going for vacation.

If you work on the seven fundamental of the fruitful family and abide in Christ who is the way and the truth and the life, you will enjoy golden anniversary. This does not necessary mean celebrating with a married partner. Remember Jesus did not have a wife. Paul doesn't tell us anything about his wife or biological children but spiritual brothers and sisters in Christ. But if you faithfully serve the Lord, he will guide you to celebration of golden anniversary. So, Mary and I when we were planning for mission to Kenya, God was using his people in Kenya in preparing for us to see the fruits of the seed which we planted many years ago.

CHAPTER 11

FRUITFUNESS GOLDEN ANNIVERSARY

Mary and I are awed by the way God has been with us for fifty years. The words which guided us when we were in courtship were: "I can do all things through Christ who strengthens me." We also owned Psalm 23 "The Lord is my shepherd; I shall not be in want." We memorized this Psalm and we like singing it during our morning devotion. We have been dumfounded by the power of the Good Shepherd. As he promises: "No one can snitch them out of my hands". Satan has tried many times and has not succeeded. He works overtime particularly when we are preparing and taking off for missions. Yet in spite of Satan's schemes, we are more than conquerors.

We are not only celebrating 50years of our life together but also the events and the seeds which we planted many years ago. Being commissioned as Church Army captain in 1964, the Captain of the first Nakuru Company of Boys and Girls Brigade (started by Presbyterian and Anglican Church), ordained Deacon in 1974; ordained priest in 1975, and establishing the first KAMA (Kenya Anglican Men Association) in 1985. Surprisingly, today there are brigade companies in Anglican, Presbyterian and Methodist churches in Kenya. There are also KAMA in most Anglican Churches in Kenya. Startlingly, during our recent mission to Kenya, we attended 20th anniversary of Thika Diocese, the ceremony started with Boys and Girls Brigade parade. All the clergy paraded in brigade uninform with Bishop Julius as the Chaplain. In 1964 we never imagined that anything of this magnitude, will occur. We were also amazed by the event which was organize by KAMA for mentoring a male child. The event was attended by males ranging from 5 to 76 years old focusing on training boys how to be men. They slaughter three goats and were taught how to prepare the meat. I never expected to see this in my life time. All the glory to God.

We got frenetic favor at All Saint Cathedral Nairobi at their thanking service. We were greeted by the Provost with: "I am the recipient of Githiga award–This is given to a student who excel on Practical Theology which Gideon and I taught at St. Paul University. St. Nicholas, which was birthed by St. Nicholas's children Home, Nakuru, sang: "plant the seed." We felt affirmed and encouraged as starters. We also launched our book: *FROM VICTORY TO VICTORY* and were commissioned by the Archbishop of Kenya as missionaries to the Global Village.

Additionally, we experienced amazing grace in the Diocese of Mount Kenya Central where we stayed in the home of Bishop Timothy and Mrs. Gichere for three days. They accorded us wonderful hospitality. We ministered about 600 clergy and their spouses, 300 lay readers and their wives and three high schools. At Kahuhia Girls (where our daughter attend for 2 years, we were given golden anniversary cake with the students putting the cake in our mouth. What a blessing. We were surprised to find ourselves with students at Muguru high school where I attended Primary Top school in 1955–56 and was a warded a gift for Character. We talked to student about Christ and Character using the motto of Booker T Washington: "Character is power." We asked the student to repeat these words several time. Interesting, it was the Head teacher of this school, Bernard Mwangi who planted the seed in me. I was seeing the radiant of God in him and made a song: "I will be saved." We had a blessing of visiting his grave. On the third day, we woke up 5.30 am so as to minister to St. James at 7am. God gave us a theme: Rejoice in the Lord always. To our surprise, the song they sung was "the joy of the Lord is my strength and Mary taught them: "Rejoice in the Lord always.

Furthermore, we had a blessing of ministering Nakuru Diocese, our canonical diocese, for three days. We minister about 500 clergy and their spouses staying in Imani center, at executive suit. We also enjoyed family reunion. We are most grateful to Bishop Dr Joseph and Mary Muchai for their love and hospitality.

Another wonder took place at Christ healing church where Patriarch was led to the church by a motor cade of eight motor cycles. We commissioned and ordained ministers and had Spirit filled service. we praise God for the ministry of Bishop John Njeru who brings together interdenominational and internationals pastors and Bishop. Bishop John prayed that God may give us long life that we may continue ministering together.

We also launched ANCCI Institute which aims at spiritual, cultural and economic transformations. The practical action by institute was donation of a pig in Embu, and three sheep to three families with an agreement that when they produce kids and piglets, the recipient will donate to a female pig or a sheep to another family. The institute also established a theological center in Thika and Embu. All glory to the Great Provider.

We are indeed grateful to all of you who have been supporting us in Prayer and financial assistance. We pray for you that you may grow in faith and to be in Christ who said: "I am the vine; you are the branches. If a man remains in me and me in him, he will bear much fruits, apart from me, you can do nothing." John 15:5.

On addition to seven fundamentals of fruitful family, you need to work hard to nurture your best self.

CHAPTER 12

NURTURE YOUR BEST SELF

In addition to being in Christ you need to nurture your best self by developing **five virtues: 1. Vision**–which is ability to see what others do not see. **Courage**-The ability to act despise fear. **Creativity**–the ability to think outside the box. **Self-confidence**– The ability to withstand criticisms. **Self-control**–The ability to delay gratification. Your young men will see vision, your old men will dream dreams.

How do the married couples get vision? In the case of Mary and me, we are given vision when we are reading the word of God and praying in Spirit. As Our loving Savior told the Samaritan woman: "God is the Spirit and his worshipers must worship him in Spirit and in truth. As Joel prophesied: "In the last days, God says, I will pour out my Spirit in all people, your sons and daughters will **prophesy**, your young men shall see **visions,** and your old men will dream **dreams**." Acts 2:17. This is all about visions. Prophecy in seeing a vision about God's will for his people and prediction of the future. The vision may come in a dream at night when we are sleeping or even during the day when we are awake.

Dr. John Githiga

My vision for Mary was a gradual process starting when she was 12-year-old when she read Isiah 5:1–8 in the family service at St. John's church, Nakuru Kenya. We were also the only teen who attended early Morning Prayer which was held from Monday to Friday. We taught children service and attend church youth meeting and youth camp where we were taught about friendship between boys and girls. We met at the home of her God parents who lived in the church compound. She was giving her sick godfather hospice care. As noted above we started the first Nakuru Boys' and Girl's Brigade together where I was the Captain and she was an Officer of Girls Brigade. I started being attracted too her because of her commitment to God and the ministry. She was also developing a feeling for me. She shared with me how they plaid a game with other girls about the first name of a young man with a vision that if she has the same number of the first name, that man is likely to be your future husband. So, John and Mary happened to have the same numbers of letters. But she was also looking for the character and the commitment to God and Ministry. So eventually we were spiritually bonding and I had to propose her in the presence of her godmother. She did not say yes or no. But we started dating. Having trained by Church Army to never let a young woman come alone to your house, we never had date in my house which was located at church compound. All our dates were held at the city park. We strongly believed that the best gift we will give to each other at our wedding was our virginity.

It is said that God does not give a vision without provision, but there is always a problem between a vision and provision. So, after dating, I reported to the priest about our friendship. Being an evangelist who was sharing the same pulpit with the priest who was jealousy of me; when I reported to the priest, without giving me a single word of advice, he reported me to our missionary Bishop, that I was dating immature girl (Mary is small in size-5' 2"–but superior in charector). When the Bishop got the information, he quickly transfer me a hundred mile away from Mary. As I later learned from his missionery friends, he did this so that our love may grow cold. However, our love for each other did not grow cold.

The Fruitful Family

Our big challenge was that the bishop went for four months leave tor Australia and Mary and I were left hanging in the air. To my great surprise, Mary's family was very supportive. My 5 years old brother in law, George said: "If they have evicted Captain John, we are going to build him a house at our backyard." My father in law comforted me with word: "When someone is playing the game, the spectators will criticize him. So do not lose heart.

When the bishop returned, I visited him. To my greatest surprise, he consented. I then asked him to be our celebrant. He agreed. I ask him to give us the date of the celebration. To my utter surprise, he said: "Mary will give us the date." I then joyfully went and asked her the best date. She gave us the date which was December 7, 1958. The bishop consented to the date.

We were amazed by God's provision for dowry, and wedding reception and honey moon. When my team visited my inlays to bargain the dowry. My first advocate was my mother in law. She said: "before you decide how much you are going to ask. Remember that Mary and John will need food after the wedding." My father in law responded: "all what I need is a pair of shoes." The team ask them to give a consent note. I was give consent even before I had bought a pair of shoes to my father in law. When we were planning for wedding reception, the team made so economical that we spent Kenya shillings 270. Which was my salary. The wedding cake was provided by a British missionary, the bridal driver was bishop's secretary who was a British. For our honey moon we were hosted by a Scottish Presbyterian missionary. He left us in his mansion with a cook who not only provided us with dinner, but also bed room coffee. We were given lot of gifts=money and utensils. And we started our live together with enough provision.

The message here for the married partners and those who are planning to marry is that you should not run way from challenges. As the Kikuyu proverb puts it: Blessing is beyond the obstacle." (Munyaka bere ya kahinga). Remember what Joseph went through after his dream-Being thrown to the ditch by his brothers and sold as a slaver and thrown to prison by Potiphar's wife. So, you need to see challengers as stepping stone, not as obstacle.

CHAPTER 13

AVOID ALL COUSES OF FAILURE IN MARRIAGE

In the following pages we are going to discuss the causes of failure in marriage and are going to draw from numerous marriage seminars I held in Kenya and my observation of failed marriages in the USA. In the marriage seminars in Kenya with the groups ranging from 20 to 700, I posed a question a question: "What spoils the relationship between a husband and wife?" The following were identified as the course of problems.

1. *Lack of premarital counseling.*

    Most young people enter into marriage without any counseling. The only information they have is what they get from their peer and the media. It has to be born in mind that marriage is one of the most complex institutions which has great impact on an individual. Your marriage partner constitutes the largest portion of your environment.

    She is the first person to see in the morning and the last person to see at night. She /he will call you more than any other person. For this reason, premarital counseling is vital.

The Fruitful Family

I do believe the one of the secrets of fruitful marriage between Mary and I is the counseling which we got from our pastor and his wife and our best man and best maid.

Moreover, the parish organized youth camps. It included the teaching on friendship between boys and girls. The teaching included "dos" and "don't s". We were taught how to value our sexuality and that the wedding cake should wait until the wedding day. That is, as the Native American was advised by her aunt, the best thing you can give to your partner is your virginity.

The Book of Common Prayer gives a good advice in this regard: "The union of husband and wife in heart, body, and mind is intended by God for their mutual joy; for the help and comfort given one another in prosperity and adversity, and, when it is God's will, for the procreation of children and their nurture in the knowledge and love of God, for the procreation of children and their nurture in the knowledge and love of the Lord. Therefore, marriage is not to be entered into unadvisedly or lightly, but reverently, deliberately and in accordance with the purpose for which it was instituted by God."

2. **Cohabitation**

Cohabit are basically self-centered and narcissistic. Their motive is "let's try and see whether it will work. My partner must prove himself/herself first. I must first eat the wedding cake." These partners are unethical and amoral. They defy customary law and Christian ethics. And this is why 99% the marriages which start with cohabitation end in divorce. During the marriage seminar we had in Nakuru, a single lady who is a lawyer argued convincingly that one of the causes of failure of the marriages today is premarital sexual intercourse. Most participants agreed with her. If you are unmarried, as it was with the Native American quoted before, the best gift you can give to your married partner is virginity. This applies to bother young men and women.

3. *Bad company*

The Kikuyu has a saying: He who accompanies a bad person becomes as bad as his companion (muchera *na mukundu a kundukaga ta guo*) If one partner or both are associating with persons who are taking drugs or alcohol or persons with divorce experience, this results in negative effect on their marriage.

4. *Separation.*

If one partner lives in the city while the other partner is in the countryside or if they live in a different country; they eventually grow a part and their marriage will end in separation. Living separately is against the will of the Creator. The creation story puts it this way: *"The Lord God said, it is not good for a man to be alone. I will make him a helper suitable for him.... So, the Lord God caused a man to fall into a deep sleep, and while he was asleep, he took one of the man's ribs and close up the place with flesh. Then the Lord made the woman from the rib he had taken out of the man, and he brought her to the man...For this reason man will leave his mother and father and be united to his wife, and they will become one flesh"* (Genesis 2:18–24). So how can the two who are one flesh live apart?

5. *Interferences–in-laws.*

As mentioned above the Bible make it clear that it is God's will for the man to leave his father and mother and cleave to his wife. Marriage is strained if one of the partners does not leave and cleave. It is even worse when the partners live in under the same roof in the same homestead with the parents. In marriage seminar which we had in California a man who sat with his wife asked: "Could you advise me on how wrestle with two bulls?" "Who are the bulls?" I asked. "My wife and my mother." Interestingly, the wife who sat with her husband didn't deny that she is one of the bulls that the man has to wrestle with. The husband's mother, a Kenyan, has moved to America so as to take care of the children. But being matriarch, she tries to assume the leadership, while the wife who is also a matriarch was unwilling to relinquish the leadership to her mother in law. The remedy to this marriage is leaving and cleaving. While the man has to honor his mother, he has to make a tough choice. While he has to support his mother, he has to cleave to his wife. For more information about this subject read my work:

Initiation and Pastoral Psychology.

6. **Weak Spirituality.**

    Another secret of failure in marriage is weak spirituality. As we have seen from the couple whom I interviewed, most of them asserted that their good relationship with God was their secret of success. Partners who are not godly, often come to a marriage relationship with expectations that God and God alone can meet. They are very much like the Samaritan woman who hopped from one man to another. She had had five husbands and Jesus revealed to her that even her present husband is not actually her husband. Marriage without God lacks the fruits of the Spirit which is: *love, peace, joy, patience, kindness, goodness, faithfulness and self–control (Galatians 5:22).*

7. **Poor Division of Labor**

    One of the secrets of failure in marriage is poor division of labor. In this case one partner is overworked while the other partner is a parasite. A large number of the people I interviewed about the secret of successes claimed that their successes were due to hard work of both of them. When I asked Jack about their secret, he summarized his answer with two words: "Hard Work." A Mexican husband told me that the secret of their success was due to hard work. He said: "I have little time for watching TV. I had to do two jobs so as to give adequate support to my family."

As loving partners, you have to share house chores. You must know exactly who the book keeper is. Who prepares for the filing of taxes? Who is in charge of cooking, serving, washing the dishes, taking out the garbage, making the bed? As was with traditional kikuyu division of labor, there were jobs which were performed by both sexes. Other jobs were done by men while others were performed by women. See my: *Initiation and Pastoral Psychology*. As St. Paul advises: "By love serves one another." "He who does not work let him not eat."

The secret of success in division of labor is letting the Spirit of God fill every fiber of our beings.

So, when the married partners put God in their lives, they will enjoy work and enjoy themselves. Interestingly work preceded the fall. Man was created for work. As the creation story puts it: "The Lord God took the man and put him in the Garden of Eden to work and take care of it" (Genesis 2:15). Not only that we were created for work, but the Creator within us gives us will and energy for doing what we are supposed to do for the family. This is what he says: *"Do you not know? Have you not heard? The Lord is everlasting God, the creator of the end of the earth. He will not grow tired or weary, and his understanding one can fathom. He gives strength to the weary and increases the power of the weak. Even youths grow tired and weary, and the young men stumble and fall; but those who love the Lord will renew their strength. They will soar with wings like eagle; they will run and not grow weary; they will walk and not faint"* (Isaiah 40:28–31).

If you are the one who is bringing stress to your partner by not doing what you are supposed to do, go to a place where you can be alone with God. Kneel down or stand and raise your hands and ask the Spirit of the living God to fall a fresh on you. Believe that God is with you and will give you strength and will of service your partner in love. He will fill your marriage with peace, love and joy and compassion.

8. *Luck of compassion*

Most of the persons who abuse their partners do so due to lack of compassion. The abuse may be physical or verbal. It can be in a form of passive aggression which employs silence as a weapon. Normally the abuser has no sympathy for his/her partner. Most of the cause of coldness is spiritual bankruptcy. It emanates from a soul without God. Thus, the secret of developing the spirit of empathy, consideration and kindness is to let God in your life.

If you are not compassionate, there is a way of developing this precious quality. Remember of an incident when your partner was in crisis. Put yourself in her shoes and cultivate the feelings to the point of tears. Do this exercise several times and then connect your feeling to your partner. You need also to remember that whenever Jesus did an act of mercy–healing and feeding–he was first moved by compassion. And thus, a Christian without compassion is a Christian without Christ. He is a contradiction in terms. Also, remember the golden rule: Do to others as you would like them do unto you. Do to your partner as you would like her/him do you. This includes allowing her/him to be and to become.

9. *Not allowing each other to be and to become.*

It has been rightly said: "no one crosses the same river twice." While there is something in personality that remains the same, there is another aspect which is constantly becoming. We are affected by our experiences and our ever-changing environment. The marriage partner who was a matriarch in the morning of their lives may become a follower in the afternoon or the twilight of their lives. The listener may become a talker while the talker may prefer to be a listener. There are also some changes which are caused by sickness. One partner may become depressed or even have a mental breakdown or may have an accident and lose a part of his body. One who had a high sex drive may have a declined sexual desire or sublimate to other activities. Most divorces occur when the major change occurs in one partner. I remember a parishioner who was in his second marriage informing me that he divorced when his wife became depressed and hospitalized. Some years later, I met him with the second wife and he quickly came to me and informed me that his second wife was having dementia.

One of Secrets of success is to embrace the new person. This includes a partner who is suffering from depression and other mental sicknesses. In marriage vows, we promise we will love, comfort, honor and keep and to hold each other: "For better for worse, for richer or poorer, in sickness and in health, to love and cherish, until we are parted by death."

As God continues working in your inner being, make every effort to appreciate your partner and vocalize your appreciation. Make this a daily routine. This practice will fill your life with peace, joy and love. It will lead to agape–love which gives and receives.

10. **One partner being a parasite**

    The other cause of failure is when one partner is **a taker**. Interesting the Kikuyu name for uninitiated boy is a taker *(kahii)*. The word Kahii also means one who takes without giving. In North American, a partner who takes without giving is known as "a dead beat." In a seminar which we held in Nakuru, violence was identified as one of the challenges facing marriage today. Surprisingly, it was noted that more women are beating up the husbands. These are particularly the husbands who are alcoholic. They are beaten by their wives when they are drunk. In a Kenyan comedy show, a husband who has lost one eye during the fight argued that the government should have a law protecting these husbands and that they should be categorized with handicapped. Of course, these husbands need treatment and rehabilitation and training for job so that they may be asset to their wives rather than a liability. If you are the one who is taking without giving, know that there is an answer to this problem. Jesus is the answer. If you if you fully commit yourself to Christ. Jesus will end the desire to beer and drug. After the being filled with the Spirit of Christ, you will be a giver rather than a taker. Remember what the Bible says: *"It is more blessing to give than to receive."* Basically, everyone has something to give. If you are in between jobs and you are not bringing any income, you can give yourself to the working partner by doing most of the house chore. By thanking her for what she is and what she is doing.

11. **Bad Habits are another cause of marriage strife.**

    This ruinous habit includes not taking care of the home, and home steads, using the utensils without washing them or even removing them from the table, being dirty and fighting over a minute thing. The couple's inability to make a conscious decision not to argue over petty things, nagging, and being critical and leaving the messes for the other to clean. They get into negative patterns of relating and fall into lazy personal habits. All these behaviors bring strife in marriage and can lead to separation and divorce.

To deal with this problem, the partners should be conscious (even if it is one partner) of the problem and make every effort to change. Christian conduct is the answer. This is summarized by Paul as: *"Whatever is true, whatever is noble, whatever is right, whatever pure, whatever is lovely, whatever is admirable–if anything is excellent or praiseworthy-think about such things"* (Philippians 4:8).

In conclusion, to avoid failure, you need three keys to success: forgiving, giving and thanksgiving. Don't go to bed with anger and unforgiving spirit. Forgive your partner even if he /she hasn't asked for forgiveness. The Bible advises us not to "let the sun go down with your anger." Our Master taught us to pray "forgive us our sin as we forgive those who sin against us." To give means to be useful to your partner. As you get out of bed, ask yourself: "how am I going to be useful to partner today? If I am only for myself; what am I and if not now when?

Show your appreciation to your partner. Do not take her for granted. Acknowledge what he/she has done. This includes the regular house chores. Praise God for gift of your partner.

Praise God for what He is and what he has done for you. Form a habit of saying the general thanksgiving together*:*

We pray, give us such an awareness of your mercies,

That with truly thankful heart we may show forth your praise,

Not only with our lips, but in our lives,

By giving up ourselves to your service,

The Fruitful Family

And by walking before you in holiness and righteousness all our days;

Through Jesus Christ our Lord, to whom, with you and the Holy Spirit,

Be honor and glory throughout all ages. Amen

(The Book of Common Prayer, New York: Church Pension Fund, 1979) p. 101

12. Private affairs (Mpango *wa Kado)*

As noted above, one of the causes of marital problem are private affairs. As I discussed with several people in Kenya about the recent bill which legalized polygamous marriage, I learned that the law makers with private affairs were the one who introduced and supported the bill. I was privileged to watch the closing argument which was broadcasted by KTN. The law maker argued: "When the first wife is coming; she must know that the second is on way; and when the second is coming, she must know that the third is in the way." This meant that the second one will come without the consent of the first wife. When this bill was signed, I became sick to the stomach. The following day I asked one of our faculty whether he would give me pastoral counseling. But he thought that I was joking because I am Chancellor and professor of pastoral counseling. I felt disorientated because the Great Mother (see my book Initiation *and Pastoral Psychology:* a chapter of Great Mother) was wounded. This was due to the fact that I have positive influence from women in my life. The first impartation came from my mother whose was called in our village, WA Gatungu (of Gatungu–Gatungu being my given name). Being named after her father she was calling me Baba (Father) when I was growing. Besides building my ego, she was very proud of her children. When my father died (I was eight years old and she was thirty years old), the local chief wanted to marry her but she refused and said: "My children will never be second class citizens." She single handedly worked so hard to raise us even during the difficult times. She succeeded in producing a Canon, a Rural Dean, two bishops who are doctors of theology and a grandson who is PhD in Engineering. She survived my father for 56 years. She was so significant to us that we gave her a title of Honorable. My two elder sisters, Jail and Mary had positive influence on me. I remember one incident when I was five years old, we were herding with Mary while a young man who was older than her approaching me. Mary thought that he was trying to hurt her brother. She hit him with a club on the forehead and the blood gushed from his face. The other incident took place when saw a woman in a form of an angel, when my friend and me were crossing Maragua River–He was nine and I was seven years old. We underestimated the flood. When we were in the middle of the river, we were being engulfed with water which was pushing us to the deep. At a nick of time, before we were totally submerged, I saw a lady holding my hand, I then held the hand of my friend, and the young woman miraculously took us to the riverbank. If this young woman had not rescued us, you could not read this book. Now you can see why I was sick when our mothers were dehumanized by the law makers in Kenya. Our augment is that women are not weak objects. This argument is supported by what I saw in Kenya in my recent mission. I saw women holding important positions in the government. I saw women in police uniforms, with machine guns protecting the country against Al–shabab. It is axiomatic that women are not weak and less tactful. KTN recently broadcasted as story of a man who was beating his wife. The wife run away but left the man with a shrinking male organ. The man was pleading with his wife publicly to come back and restore his sexual organ.

Another example of women's strength is demonstrated by, Meriam Ibrahim, who was condemned while eight months pregnant, to be flogged a hundred time and then to be executed for Marrying a Christian man, while her dad who abandoned them when she was a child, was a Muslim. She was put in a prison cell with her twenty-month Martin, awaiting to deliver and then be flogged and hanged. She stood firm in Christ and was ready to die for her marriage and her faith in Christ. She was forsaken by her brothers. One of her brothers said: "it's one of two; if she repents and returns to our Islamic faith and to the embrace of our family, then we are her family and she is ours, 'but if she refuses, she should be executed.'"

Meriam experienced great pain for not only being forsaken by her family, but also giving birth in shackles. Yet she stood firm in her faith in Christ and her husband Wani. Her heroine action became global. Amnesty International condemned the sentence against Ibrahim, calling it 'abhorrent,' and the U.S. State Department said it was 'deeply disturbed' by the sentence. Finally, due to international pressure, Merian was released and flew to Italy with Italia Airlines, and had a blessing of shaking hands with Pope Francis.

When we honor women, we honor our mothers and sisters and ourselves. We respect that part of ourselves which I term *Great Mother* which creates and repairs human relationships. She helps us to reach out, to join and get in touch with, and be involved in concrete feelings, things and people. She is the source of life and nourishment. It is our prayer that our mothers and sisters will be emancipated. We also pray that Kenya will have strong prophetic voices and strong Christian politicians who will have this barbaric law repealed. As we have argued, the Bible makes it clear that marriage is between one man and one woman. It is also unhealthy for one partner to have extramarital sexual intercourse. The partners must be faithful to each other whether they have children or not.

It would be unfair to end this section without speaking for husbands. In the above-mentioned seminar which was held in Nakuru, Kenya, it was reported that there are more wives who are beating their husbands. They particularly beat them when they are drunk. This action is not justifiable. Alcoholism is a decease and for that reason the man needs rehabilitation and treatment. The church needs to have a group which is trained in intervention which would help the family in convincing the man to join Alcoholic Anonymous. Being a father of many nations, I have dealt with the causes of abused husband by the wives of different nations. Among the Mexicans who were members of the church, women who were in leadership fought or kicked their husbands when they were unemployed or were unable to bring enough money. One parishioner told me that his wife repeated the words "you have to go," so often that his five-year son would say to him: "Dad, you have to go, but I love you." Finally, when the wife's financial situation improved, the man was expelled from the house.

Among the African Americans whom I passionately ministered for twelve years, generally speaking, husbands were treated as eternal boys. At one time I called a man who was a parishioner, when he picked the phone, the wife who held the other phone was the first to answer for her husband and would not even allow the husband to speak with his pastor.

Wives of the Sudanese in diaspora whom we have ministered with lot of dedication and self-sacrifice, routinely call the police whenever there is a conflict between them and their husband. Whoever this happens, it is the husband who is handcuffed. As I write this page, Mama Mary has just given pastoral care to our priest who was visited by the police as he was just leaving for the church. His wife who is psychotic and has moved to another state called the police and lied to them that his husband was molesting his children. Before they had to handcuff him, he informed them that the woman is insane, and he showed them the court order which forbade the mother from being closer to the children. If this innocent husband didn't have the letter from the court, he could have been booked and leave behind the children whom he dearly loves.

In Western Kenya, it is reported that women in power are routinely raping men. There was a story which was reported in the local media of a male student who was given a ride by a lady. When he entered the car, he was given a snack. Instead of being taken to his destination, he was taken to a hotel. By the time they reached the hotel, the young man was drugged. The woman spent a night with the boy and left him alone, drugged with his sexual organ still erected. The boy was taken to the hospital by the police women who deal with these cases of the boys who are raped by women.

The above illustrations surface to show that many husbands are victims. As we have argued for husbands who are the head of their family, women in leadership should honor and love their husbands as Christ loved the church despite of its imperfection. When they let Christ in their lives, they will have Christ's love. This is what Jesus says about this love: "My commandment is this: Love each other as I have loved you. Great love has no one like this that he lays down his life for his friends." When father is dehumanized, the community lose vital qualities which are the substance of the Great Father. These qualities include wisdom, initiative, assertiveness, creativity and objectivity. (For more information see *Initiation and Pastoral Psychology* in a chapter about the Great Father). Married partners with this love will embrace each other whether they have children or not.

13. Children

Children or lack of them can bring strain in marriage. When the couple stay without a child, there is pressure both from them and the extended family. When children come, they can also be potential source of problem. Each partner comes with different family experiences, blessing and taboos. At a time, the differences while they are a source of conflict, they are also complementally. Nj?. For instance, to rear a balance person, there is a need for control and freedom. One parent may be a dispenser of control while the other sees freedom as an ideal. The other area of conflict is support. One parents may regard the highest support as an ideal while the other prefer less support. The parents who have these opposing attitudes need to know that the children require bother freedom and control. If a child is over-controlled, the ego is weakened and will have problem to function is the society. If they have no control at all, they may become delinquents. Thus, the parents need to give each other freedom and make every effort to balance each other. However, having children can bring additional stress into a marriage because caretaking of children requires more responsibility as well as a change in roles, provides more fodder for disagreement and strain, and reduces the amount of time available for bond as a couple.

How to be a blessing to yourself and to the children.

i. Have time alone. This is the time when you enjoy each other and make the rules of how discipline and rear the kids and to enjoy yourself.

ii. Respect each other's view point remembering that each method has a positive effect on Children.

iii. When children try to separate you remind them: Your mom is my wife and the Bible advises you to honor your mother and father-This is a commandment with a promise that you will live well on earth. I am also admonished that I should love my wife as Christ loves the church. Your Dad is my husband the Bible requires that I love him and you are advised to honor and obey him.

iv. Be firm but not too serious with your children. Have fun and pray and read the Word of God with them.

Do realize that children were created with free will and one of their desires is to be different from their parents. They like occupying the empty space.

v. Know that like a prodigal son, they go through lostness particularly during their teenage (see *Initiation and Pastoral Psychology*—a chapter on lostness. When this is taking place remember a Swahili proverb: *asiyepotea haijui njia*—He who does not get lost does not know the way.

vi. Do not blame each other because of the shortcoming of your children. Remember David, the King after God's heart had Amon who raped his sister and Absalom who tried to overturn his father's government. Monica had Augustine who following the wrong company but later became one of the Church fathers, a Bishop and a Saint.

vii. If you don't have children. Adopt. The adopted children may even be more bonded to you than biological children. Remember Jesus was adopted by Joseph.

viii. Be contented with each other and with your children. As Saint Paul puts it: contentment with godliness is a great gain. *"And we know that in all things God works for good of those who love Him, who has been called according to His purpose"* (Romans 8:28).

CHAPTER 14

FAMILY IN A TECHNOLOGICAL SOCIETY

Rearing children in a technological society poses great challenge to the married partners. The couples and their counsellors should bear in mind that personality is shaped by three factors:

1. Heritage. This include the genes of the parents and ethnic cultural heritage which is embedded in mythology, language of the tribe which is sub-symbolic universe of meaning of the tribe.

2. Environment. This include home, school, church, mass media, peer pressure. The media will include phonography, information about how to get drug and alcohol and how to join terror groups. Parents cannot fully control their children from media.

3. Self-determination—Humans were given freedom of choice. As someone has puts it "we are condemned to make choices." Remember even if you decide not to make a choice; you have made a choice. As Adler puts it: "You are either moving

toward useful or useless destination." When teen decide to take drugs, they are traveling toward useless destination. This brings stress in marriage. The married partners need to hold hands together instead of blame game.

Those in diaspora do have extra challenges in that an individual is overprotected–you cannot use a cane. The proverb: "spare the rod spoil the child," is irrelevant in USA.

Children know their rights before they know how to become responsible. The consequence is prolonged adolescence. Children continue being a burden to their parents until late in their twenties. Others may remain deadbeat for life. In this case, the married partners should continue to love one another and to talk to and pray for their children without enabling their bad habit by giving them money.

As a Diaspora, bear in mind that if your children were born in Western Hemisphere, they speak the language without accent. By having accent, they may think that they are more sophisticated in the western way of life than their parents. As a parent don't feel inferior. But remember your children don't have the blessings of facing challenges which you went through when you were growing Your Character was built by poverty, Hunger, war, safe and unsafe environments. This build up your character and in the words of Booker T Washington: "Character is power."

Lack of puberty rite of passage which enabled teens to move from childhood to adulthood contributes to postmodern problems which is characterize by additions, teen pregnancy, tattoos, bad behavior and wasting of time. Adolescence is one of the most challenging stage in life. Wayne Rise has written a book which is entitled *"HELP! THERE IS A TEENAGER* IN THE HOUSE." Teenage is a challenge to both the teens and their parents. They experience tension between childhood and adulthood; Independence VS dependence; Adolescent and his/her pear group; ethics and sexual urges; self-identity VS role confusion. (For more information see. John Githiga: Initiation and Pastoral Psychology. Amazon.com)

Being different personality types, the parents are challenged differently. One parent may be a dispenser of freedom while the other install discipline; one parent my pay attention to ideal and what the child has not become; while the other focuses on the growing edge. While each of these opposing attributes are useful to the child, they bring tension between the married partners. Father and mother should equip themselves with three keys to success: forgiving; thanksgiving; giving. They have to forgive each other and forgive their children. The partners need to consistently appreciate one another and compliment their children for whatever they do. As the couple who whose secret of success is fifty, fifty, each partner must work hard to support the family. Children need to be trained to do their chores. These will train them to be contributing members of the family and the society.

You also need to continue instructing and guiding your children. Do not turn your home to a war zone. Choose your battle carefully—don't burn your energy with small thing. It is not a big deal when a teen doesn't come to the dinner table on time.

More importantly, as parents, have time for yourself—discuss how you are going to deal with the children realizing that there are things which are beyond your control and beyond their control. Love one another, love your children. Once again Paul reminds us: "Love is patient and kind; it is not easily angered; it keeps no records of wrong, it always protects, always trust, always hope, and always persevere." I Corinthian 13:4–7

Just as there are many programs for destroying the family, the are also made program for building up. Our home, in the living room, we turn on Gospel songs. We have Southern Sudan Gospel songs; Easter African Gospel songs, Kenya Gospel songs, Kikuyu Gospel song. In the bedroom we have Christian radio which include Ezra Radio which is run by Dr John and Dr Naum Mwaniki. When we get in the car, we either turn Christian radio or put on Gospel CD. We praise the Lord for the availability of these programs.

Dr. John Githiga

IT IS NOT ALL YOUR FAULTS

AS A PARENT, YOU NEED to bear in mind that when your children deviate from the right path, it is not all your fault. You need to know that the human being is shaped by 1. parents 2. environment and 3. self-determination.

humans draws from parents, environment and self-determination. I am so startled by the way Our family draw from our parents, and great parents. From my paternal grandfather who was a diviner,(traditional psychologist and psychotherapist, I have insatiable desire of studying the psychology, sociology and cultural anthropology. From my maternal grandfather (Gatungu) who was specialized in removing family curses. I became a blesser. I like ending my communication with word: "God bless you." From my father, who was a teacher, preacher, community developer. All the family member have carried forward the family mission. My brother Gideon taught and wrote books but also became the first Bishop of Thika where he started economic investment program and by the time he retired, the program had over one billion Kenya shilling. This was impartation from our father who started community development by introducing planting cash crops such plums, apples, tea plantation and cider trees.

ENVIRONMENT is another influence. The environment include, school, media, and the church. Children and youth can easily get to wrong company through the telecommunication. Both the church and parents need to guide the children to watching the right programs. As I have mentions, in our family we like listening to Gospel music, watching Christian channels in TV and turning on Christian radio in our car.

Finally, humans are created with freedom of choice. As someone has said human were condemned to make choices, and are hundredth present responsible for the choices which they make. The good news is that if we accept Christ, He will guide us to fruitful path for he is the way and the truth and life. Thus, if the family is led by Christ everyone will play his part in the family. And by love, they will serve one another, the church and the community.

CHAPTER 15

DIVISION OF LABOR IN THE FAMILY

Professor John Mbiti rightly state African Ontology is I am because we are and since we are therefore." Since one was begotten as and to a community, responsibility to the community took priority over the service to an individual. An individual was first and foremost responsible to the nuclear family, which included parents, brothers, sisters, and half-brothers and half-sisters. By the same token, he worked for the extended family, which included grandparents, uncles, aunts, nieces, and nephews.

On addition to performing duties for the family, every person rendered some duty to his or her age group and gave assistance to the members of his clan. In most cases, this assistance was in the form of hospitality. For example, a wealthy man could allow a poor clan member to cultivate a portion of his land and put up a homestead.

Not only was an individual obligated to his or her primary groups, but every individual had territorial responsibilities. Every man and woman had definite duties to all the members of the village. These duties included fortification, protection and defense of the village. If called upon, he could also assist his neighbor in erecting a house, clearing the bush, and cultivating. A neighbor could count on sufficient assistance to build a house in a day or clear a large area for cultivation in a few days, without having to pay for the labor, except that he must supply the workers with a feast. He must also have initiated the work himself as a proof that he was not looking for help because he was lazy. He must also be someone who assists others. He who does not assist others is left alone with a proverb: "He who eats alone, dies alone."

When the expectant mother delivers, the neighboring women set a date on which they bring firewood, porridge, cooked food, sorghum, mallet, corn, sugar cane, sweet potatoes, and yams to the mother. In most cases, the mother of the newly born could get fuel and food supplies enough for three months. This gave her ample time for regaining her energy and nursing her baby without worrying about food and firewood for her family. Furthermore, an individual was a part of and responsible to the whole country. Duties to one's country included defense, building of bridges, and firefighting.

Another major responsibility that every citizen had was related to religion. In time of drought, plague, and other calamities, the leading elders summoned all the people to gather together for worship. They then congregated under the Tree of God and gave sacrifice to the Great Provider. When killing the sacrificial animal, a boy, a girl, and a woman who has gone through menopause touched the animal's head while the elders slaughtered it and prepared and roasted the meat. This was a symbolic act of inclusiveness and the community's total participation in the religious act. They then invoked the Ancient of the Day, a God who was worshiped by people of both sexes and of all ages. It was believed that faithful worship resulted in God's blessings for all. The blessing included gifts of rain, good harvest, health, unity, peace and prosperity, and vitality and capability of carrying out various responsibilities.

Customarily, there were duties that were performed by males and those which were done by females, as well as those which were wrought jointly by both sexes. Duties had nothing to do with the demonstration of superiority or inferiority, weakness or strength. Some of the jobs that were performed by women were too difficult for men. For instance, the Kikuyu women were trained (not by men but by women) from childhood to lift and carrying heavy things, such as firewood, in such a way that they built their muscles and were able to lift and carry heavier loads than men. This sounds awkward to the Western people. An American classmate and a great friend of mine shouted at me, "Shame on you!" for telling him that my mother could lift heavier objects than myself. He couldn't imagine how a fifty-eight-year-old woman could carry a heavier load than a man of thirty-four years of age.

A Kikuyu woman is not perceived by a Kikuyu male as psychologically or physically weak. Neither does she regard herself as a weaker object. There is a feeling of democracy and equality between the opposite sexes. This equality is not only evident in the division of labor, but also in the naming system. This is why children are named equally after paternal and maternal lineage. For instance, in our family, we are six. Three of us are matrilineal while the other three are patrilineal.

1. **Man's duty**

    As we have seen, during the weaning rite, the boy was made aware that he was growing to be a warrior. Hence, every Kikuyu male was a soldier. Military recruitment started after the initiation. The young man started by being a member of the junior regiment. At this initial stage, he had no direct responsibility or power. He was under the authority of the senior warrior regiment. After several years of training, he was promoted to the senior warrior regiment.

    Apart from being a soldier, the male was a farmer. Men's work included cultivating the virgin land, bulldozing huge trees, cutting thick and thorny bushes, and working in the male gardens in which they grow male plantations, such as sugar canes, bananas, yams, tobacco, and sweet potatoes.

Additionally, men rolled or carried logs and heavy wood for erecting houses, building a bridge, or for fortification of a village. They guarded the family and domestic animals against wild animals and the poachers from other tribes.

The elderly men and boys took animals to the pasture. It was also a male's duty to slaughter, roast, and distribute meat to the members of the family. They prepared and treated hides, which were used for making clothes, baby carriers, and beds. Metal work, carpentry, wood carving, and the making of bee hives were men's duties. They made superior spears, arrows, shields, and other ammunition, which were used by the warriors and also sold to the neighboring tribes, such as Masai and Wakaba.

2. **Woman's duty**

A Kikuyu woman was tutored and trained for domestic and field work from the earliest stage of her life. As we have seen, during the weaning rite, the mother took the girl to the field where the latter ritually worked in the farm and carried small bundles of firewood. These were symbolic actions indicating that she was growing to work both in the house and in the field.

As it was with males, every female was an agriculturist. A married woman had her own farm and a granary storage. She had to produce enough food for her family and have a surplus, which she would take to the market so as to buy other commodities were needed by the family.

In addition, women made a variety of earthenware, such as cooking pots and containers for alcoholic beverages, water, and grain. They weaved bags and baskets of numerous sizes, which were used for carrying grains, glossary, and other articles. They also plastered the walls of the house with clay and cow dung and painted it with white wash.

3. **Duties performed by both sexes**

After initiation, there were more interactions between males and females. They feasted and socialized together. Since work was experienced as the celebration of life and socialization, there were some jobs which were performed jointly by men and women.

For instance, while men cultivated thick and thorny bushes, both sexes joined hands in breaking the ground, planting, weeding, and harvesting. Likewise, when erecting a house, the males did all the woodwork while women thatched the roof with the grass, but they both plastered the walls with mud.

Trading and commerce were done by both males and females. Women sold and bought grains, earthenware, bags, and baskets, while men traded in domestic animals; working tools; weapons such as spears, bows, arrows and shields; and all wood and metal products. Both sexes and all ages participated in religious activities. These activities nurtured the inner and objective Tree of God and enhanced the community's harmony and cohesiveness.

4. **Religious duties**

For the Kikuyu, as it is with other African people, religion was *sine qua non* to human life. Just as one cannot exist without air, water, and food, one cannot do without religion. Hence, it is axiomatic that every individual and the entire creation must participate in religious duties, worship, and ceremonies. It is impossible to perform any political, social, or military services without being involved in a religious ritual of some kind, because religion is life and life is religion. It permeates in all the departments of human life so fully that it is impossible to isolate it. If a person refuses to cooperate in important religious rituals, he is forced by the family and neighbor to undergo through the rite. For instance, if a young man refuses to be circumcised, he is circumcised by force. Even in the modern technological society, if the Kikuyus discover that a particular man is not circumcised, they plot and confound him, and circumcise him by force. They'd rather risk to be imprisoned than to permit a male to stay uncircumcised.

5. **Political duties**

- Junior warrior regiment

    After the initiation the male became not only a full-grown person and a he-man but he also became a responsible member of society. His developmental title changed from kihii, a recipient or he-who-stretches-his-palm-to-receive to mwanake, my-son-take-the-weapon. He had to take the weapon and join the junior warrior regiment. His father gave him the armaments, which included a spear, a shield, and a sword. He was also provided with a sheep or a goat, which he used as fees to the warrior regiment school and a sacrifice to God. The animal was used for the ceremony, which entered the young man into warriorhood. His weapons were sprinkled with the blood of the sacrificial animal by the elder. He took an oath of allegiance and then the warriors feasted on the meat and then held a mock fighting.

    After the ceremony, the junior warrior could go to war but had no power or authority. He was subordinate to the authority of the senior warriors and had no direct responsibilities. He acted as an acolyte or a server. Senior warrior regiment.

The Fruitful Family

After eighty-two moons, the junior warrior was promoted to senior warrior. He gave two goats or sheep as a fee for the rite of passage. the feast was followed by a big dance in which the warrior was permitted to dance in the inner circle. The ceremony ushered him to specific responsibilities and granted him the powers that go with the duties. He had authority over the junior warriors.

The regiment was governed by the councils. Territorially, there were village councils, district councils and the national council. Each of the councils was presided over by an elected president. The election of the presidents or judges was by consensus. There was no casting of votes. The leader was someone who possesses the spirit and the ideal of the community. He mirrored the ideals and aspirations of the group and had selfless dedication to the course of the village and national councils. He had to be someone who had demonstrated leadership qualities, impartiality in justice, bravery in war and discipline in a group.

The group leader represented his group to the village council; the village president represented the village to the district council, while the presidents of the district councils formed the national council of warriors. The leader of the warriors' councils also presented the interest of the young people to the elder's councils.

- The rite of passage to the senior eldership

As we have noted, the puberty rite was both a rite of passage for both the initiate and his or her parents. The initiate became a woman and a man while the parents were promoted to senior eldership. The parent moved from the stage of young adulthood to mature adulthood. The father moved from the state of a weapon-bearer to the bearer-of-the-sacred-leaves, from wearing the "military uniform" to wearing religious and political vestments (matathi). The mother moved from the state of being Kangei, young plant, to mature womanhood, Nyakinyua.

In this regard, when one had a boy or girl who was old enough to be circumcised, he was approached by the senior elders and was asked to prepare himself for the rite which was known as Gutonyio Keri, to be entered the second time, or the second rite of passage, which was to make him a bearer-of-the-sacred-leaves and the staff of the office. After getting the message from the senior elders, he consulted with the shaman. The shaman advised him about the right day for the occasion. The candidate then informed the village elders about the day a week before the appointed day.

In the morning of this day, the senior elders came and sat in the circle outside the house of the senior wife, who brought them food and drinks. Then the elders appointed two elders, who were to officiate the rite. Carrying their sacred leaves and staffs of office, the two elders entered the house and found the man and his wife seated at the fireplace. They prayed and blessed them. The rite of passage conjoined the candidates with their genesis and then reintroduced to tribal philosophy, which was embodied in idioms, proverbs, riddles, stories, and wise sayings. After that they chanted a prayer to God for the child who was about to be circumcised:

> O, Ancient of the Day, the Ageless elder,
> God of our fathers, help our child to be successfully
> to grow in knowledge and in stature,
> to prosper and to bear many healthy children
> so as to perpetuate the family line.
> Glory be to the Great Provider
> and peace to our children."

The Fruitful Family

After the prayer, the man and his wife were sworn by the two elders to keep confidentiality of the senior elder's council. After this, the man was led out by the elders, walking between them, followed by his wife. The four entered into the circle and the man who had now become a senior elder greeted the elders, "My equal," (Wanjuwakine) and the elders responded in unison, "Our equal." After this, the wife returned to the house and brought a calabash of beer. She was also assisted by other senior women to bring food to the elders. The elders slaughtered a he-goat and dipped it's sexual organs into the blood and tied it on his wrist. This symbolized the fact that "Our equal" will never again be influenced by Eros in making judgments, but will be led by logos, which was embodied in Kikuyu's idioms, proverbs, and wise sayings. Henceforth, he must be led by reason and wisdom and not by passion and pursue truth and justice at any cost.

After the ritual, the elder ate the roasted meat and drink the beer all the day long. From then on, the man who had become a senior elder never again greeted other senior elders in the usual, "Wi mwega," (How is it?), but "Wanyuwakini," (My equal, or He who belongs to you at equal basis). These forms of greetings were solely reserved for those who were religiously, politically, and socially equal—the bearers of the sacred leaves and staffs of the office-athuri a matathi. (the elders who carry the sacred leaves)

The duties of the senior elder included the study of Kikuyu philosophy and statues, peace-making, conflict management, advising the junior elders, attending senior elder's councils, offering sacrifices to God, and communicating with ancestors.

Since all the senior elders were equal, the Kikuyu did not have high priests, kings, but they had judges, who presided over the councils. A judge (Muthanaki) was a person who had leadership qualities, had demonstrated bravery in war, impartiality in judgment, devoted to the ideals of the community, was respected, and was taken seriously by all people. He was the most competent and diligent man in the age set and was capable of perceiving and articulating what was in the mind of the people. He had the audacity of and has mastered the whole gamut of people's political, social, and religious systems.

Even though the president was revered, he was not necessarily the wealthiest man. Unlike the modern westernized political leaders who buy their leadership and take it by the point of a gun, a traditional leader never bought his position with material things. He never campaigned and bribed people in order to win an election. By the same token, he never received bribery as to favor a particular person. He was elected because of his integrity and wealth of knowledge of people's democratic systems, which was based in circumcision and which stressed the individual's freedom to life, liberty, and property ownership with the full understanding that the government was by and for and of the people. He was aware that he was only first among equals and that his task was to create an atmosphere whereby justice could roll down like waters, and righteousness like an ever-flowing stream. The Kikuyu democracy was more inclusive than that of the ancient Greeks. For unlike the Greek republic, which excluded women, aliens, and slaves from politics, the Kikuyu democracy embraced all those who were circumcised, regardless whether they were rich or poor.

As noted, people governed themselves through the councils. The first grade was the junior warrior's council, which was comprised of unmarried young men and women. The second grade was the senior warrior's council, which was composed of those who were married but did not have children and

The Fruitful Family

who were old enough to be circumcised. Young men, who belonged to this council, were known as spear-bearers and their councils was known as the council of weapon bearers. They were young fathers, who were still in the military. The female members of this council were known as young plants (Kangei). The role of this council was enforcement of community ethics to themselves and their juniors. They also congregated in the evenings for socializing, mutual friendly confrontation and brainstorming.

The third grade was the senior elder's council. This was for those elders, who carry the sacred leaves. This council dealt with important social, political, economic and religious issues.

Territorially, there were villages, local districts and country-wide councils. The senior elders' village councils included all men in the village who had been initiated to senior eldership and their wives and the presidents of junior and senior warriors' councils. The presidents of the warrior councils were allowed to speak only when they had to present cases of the warriors. Otherwise, they were expected to sit and listen to the elders, so as to learn how to deal with judicial deliberations when they became senior elders.

The presidents of the village councils formed the district council, while the presidents of district councils formed the country-wide council, which assembled at the Kikuyu's "Garden of Eden" (Mukurwe wa Gathanga) whenever there were national issues.

Interestingly, Kikuyu democracy permitted the jurors to express both the unstructured and structured spheres of the psyche. When everyone had assembled, the president asked the elders to blow up or let the steam out (Kwibebeukia). Then they had a brief episode whereby everyone said whatever was on his mind and whatever was said at that time must go with the wind and could never be cited during the deliberation. After this episode, the judge then called the council into order. During this phase, everyone must be rational, logical, and must demonstrate integrity. The decisions were made by consensus. The Kikuyu, as it was with other African people, valued human relationships more than resolutions. In modern Kenya, modernized things are more prized than humanity. That being the case, most of the political leaders are elected because of their monetary possessions. After gaining power, which is without authority, they dip their fingers into the pockets of their electors. These poor politics have had bad effects on the economy, home, and family life. Kenya, as with other countries in Africa, south of the Sahara, has been politically shaken by colonization and decolonization. Colonization superimposed the West's political system on the continent, while decolonization left a mixture of African socialization and Western political systems. Africa, south of the Sahara, is in a liminal entity, between ethnocentricity and nationality, traditionality and modernity. As we shall see in the following pages, the family's aircraft is flying in the turbulent atmospheric conditions of change. Yet, we strongly believe that even though there are dying elements, a very healthy child will be borne by this continent, which is the mother of all humanity.

A. DIVISION OF LABOR AND FAMILY IN TRANSITION

THE DIVISION OF LABOR IN Kenya and Africa, south of the Sahara, has to be observed against the background of dichotomies experienced by the modern African. There are dichotomies between tradition and modernity, urbanization and ruralization, literacy and illiteracy, Christianity and Islam versus traditional religions. and nationalization, traditional political systems and political idealisms borrowed from the Western hemisphere, African social systems and the growing social stratification that is being adopted from the West, and authoritarianism and absolution versus African freedom of expression, which was fostered by the age-grouping systems.

The Africans are somewhat hovering in the air looking for firm ground on which to settle. They are between time. There is something that is ebbing, declining, dying, and decaying. Nevertheless, a fully developed embryo is vibrating, breathing, and kicking in the African womb. Its name, nature, form, and character are unknown.

I perceived this fetus when I was conducting marriage seminars in various places in Kenya in 1970s-1980s. The group ranged from thirty to five hundred. The questions for discussion were: *What spoils the relationship between a husband and a wife today? What should the marriage partners do to improve their relationship?* The groups identified a number of issues that were affecting an individual's role in the family and society. It was observed that we are moving from a patriarchal society to a matriarchal society, or democratization of the genders; children who were traditionally the parent's assets and wealth are now becoming liabilities; the husbands who were ever in the homesteads in the father's house are migrating from the homesteads to the cities and towns, leaving their wives in the countryside with the disproportional burden of family care; alcoholic beverages, which were customarily taken during special celebrations, have become daily drinks for men and women who are suffering from spiritual emptiness; drugs, which were unheard of by our forefathers, are becoming rampant; money and the economy is changing both the philosophy of life and concept of time; and the marriage partners and single parents who have careers have left their children in the hands of teenage-maids.

1. **Movement from a patriarchal society to a matriarchal society**

    As we have seen, initiation introduced a democratic system in the family and community. The father was, however, the chairman or head of the family. The mother, on the other hand, was trained from childhood on how to turn the "head." To use the words of the Mother's Union, she was the "neck" of the "head." She was a strong backbone of her husband. She tactfully and unconsciously turns the "head." But all of a sudden, she has become a "neck" without a "head." The "head" has moved from the homestead in the rural areas to the city for salaried jobs. Some fathers visit their families once a month, others once a year, while some never come back home. Research, which was conducted by Nairobi University, estimated that 60 percent of the husbands in Kenya are absentee husbands.

Some husbands who stay with their families tend to ignore domestic responsibility if their wives are professional with better salaries than the husbands. As one wife complained during the marriage enrichment seminar, "Although my husband has a job, I am totally responsible for the family. Not only do I have to feed, clothe and educate the children, but I also have to feed and clothe my husband. At first, I was outraged, since I never saw my mother playing this role. But I gradually regarded my husband as one of my boys. This conviction gave me a peace of mind. Nevertheless, it gets on my nerves, whenever he shouts at me." Thus, most wives are both the breadwinners and the managers of their home. It is estimated that two-thirds of the grains in Africa, south of the Sahara, is produced by women.

A few young husbands, particularly those who are brought up by the single mothers, have accepted the leadership of their wives. As one young man said to his fiancé during premarital counseling: "I was brought up by my mother. She was the head of the family. I don't know what it is for a man to be the head of the family and for that reason, don't expect me to head our family. Lead and I will follow."

However, even if the husband or the wife accepts his position, this does not always solve the problem, since one sphere of the family is patriarchal. A wife with an irresponsible husband may have a neighboring family with a very responsible husband and she may constantly compare her condition with that of her neighbor and thereby suffer from a relative deprivation.

2. **Children are becoming liabilities**

Customarily, children were regarded as a great asset by the parents because of the fact that they constituted the work force. After becoming grown up, they performed domestic work, cared for livestock, and worked in the farm. The young warriors raided other tribes and captured their cattle, goats, and sheep, which they brought to their parents. The young women were given for marriage and the parents received the bride's prize in return. Currently, the parents are financially supporting their children (without receiving anything in return) until they are through with their primary, secondary and college education. Since the parent's regard educated children as a great investment, they rid them of any duty that could interfere with their studies. The parents from middle and upper classes employ house maids to do all the chores so as to allow their children to give their undivided loyalty to academic work. They do this with the anticipation of getting a lion's share in economic benefits, which their children will attain after graduating from college and are employed in well-paying jobs. On the contrary, by being over-indulged and ever-receiving from the parents without reciprocating, some modern young adults have become eternal parasites to their parents. They continue making heavy demands on their family, even after getting employment. Some have sued their aging fathers so as to force them to relinquish the family property to them. The first born of a lay-reader of a church that I ministered at in Kenya filed a lawsuit against his father alleging that his father was an alcoholic and was intending to sell his land through the influence of alcohol. The young man wanted the court to authorize the transfer of the title deed to him. However, his father, who only sipped wine once a week during the Holy Communion, was found innocent. But he was terribly hurt by being sued by his son, whom he has reared and educated. In some cases, the fathers have been murdered by their pampered sons as they attempted to acquire their father's property. Thus, children who were their parent's life insurance in the past have become unbearable monsters. These parasites have depleted and exhausted their parents. They have broken their hearts and have inflicted a sharp, thin pain in their guts.

3. **Interferences from in-Laws**

   According to the passing generation, a young man built a house away from his parents before or after marriage. Never did he live in the same homestead with his parents after marriage. This set-up enabled him to build a separate and independent nuclear family.

   Presently, due to scarcity of land, some young couples live in the same homestead and use the same gate with their parents. In addition to that, some wealthy parents employ their sons to either work in their farms or operate their business. Consequently, these parents regard their sons and daughter-in-law as their possession. If the daughter-in-law is a career woman, the "big daddy" expects her earnings to come to the main pool. If the son leaves for work in the town and stays away from his family, the "big daddy" may become a "big husband" to his daughter-in-law and have an affair with her—a behavior which was regarded as an outrageous incest taboo in the old days.

During the marriage seminars, the young wives who were victims of the systems, expressed their resentments with the following statements, "Never shall I accept to be absorbed by the in-laws." "I have no problem with my husband, but I am constantly offended by his father's interference and authoritarianism." "Unless my husband moves away from that homestead," lamented a young woman who had returned to her parents, "I shall never go back to that home." "My husband forms a coalition with his parents against me," complained a young school teacher. "I am tired, fed-up, and burnt out for using too much energy in self-defense. I cannot stand it anymore." These women felt over-worked, exploited, and abused. The situation may worsen if the husband moves to the city for job opportunity and leaves his wife and children in the countryside.

4. **Absentee husbands and division of labor**

Customarily, a husband lived in a hut, which was situated in the homestead near the main gate in order to guard the family and the livestock. There, his children went for advice. His wives visited him for sexual gratification. But the bad news is that westernization, urbanization, and job opportunities have moved the father's house from the homestead to the city. As we have noted, some husbands come home once a month, others once a year, and others after a decade, while others never come back home. This phenomenon of absentee husbands is prevalent in Africa, south of the Sahara. It is also a trend in the West Indies. During my visit to Barbados, I learned that most husbands are either in the United Kingdom or the United States for job opportunities. They leave their wives and children on the Island, and in most cases, the husband never comes back home. The mother has to provide, protect, and guide her children. It is also estimated that 70 percent of the African

American families in the United States are headed by a mother. The mother is not only the head of the household, but she is also the provider. In some cases, the African American mother is over-worked, burnt out, depleted, and battered. The African American father does not voluntarily abandon his family responsibility, but has been forced by the evil forces, which have been afflicting him for over three hundred years. No father's ego has been as severely mutilated as the black father's in the United States. Even though he has made enormous contributions in the American society, in science and technology, being the mayors of major cities, being American ambassadors to the United Nations, being the top soldiers (like Colin Powell), being the judge of the Supreme Court (like Clarence Thomas), being innovators and discoverers—he is still regarded as the embodiment of evil. He is witch-hunted more than any other human. Society puts a magnifying glass on his birthmark or his blind spots and turn a blind eye to the superior side of his personality. He never hears anything positive either about himself or his father land. The media tells him constantly that he's in prison, on drugs, a murderer, irresponsible, and accused of other vices. The harder he endeavors to humanize humanity, the more he is dehumanized; the more he enriches the society, the more he is impoverished; the more he protects, the more he is attacked; the more he tries to build, the more his ego is demolished. The African American father is a victim who is regarded as and punished as a criminal. He is, indeed, caricatured and then lynched. His suffering is the suffering of the black mother and her family.

For when he is psychologically incapacitated, he strikes the nearest and the safest object—the black mother. Statistically, there are more black wives, who are beaten up by their husbands than white wives. They beat them because of low-self-esteem, which is inflicted on them by

The Fruitful Family

the society and pent-up anger generated from work and social environments. By being smothered from childhood to adulthood by the Great Black Mother, the black male's avenues to responsible partnerships are blocked. And, thus, the black mother has to shoulder all the family's burden.

Nevertheless, we have "seven thousand black fathers" who have triumphantly liberated themselves from the status of eternal boyhood. They have allowed their roots to penetrate deeper to their fatherland thereby drawing ego energy from the African Great Father and Great Mother. They have stretched their alms over the Atlantic Ocean and have reached out to Ethiopia, their mother land. Rather than being ashamed of being identified by their motherland, they are proud of their heritage. These fathers are responsible marriage partners. They are sought after as precious jewels for political, societal and ecclesiastical leadership. They are the messiahs of the African American boys. And since they knew where the shoe pinches, they are nurturing the egos of these boys and are helping them to travel on the road that leads to responsible manhood. By re-Africanizing, humanizing, and Christianizing these black males, the "seven thousand black fathers" are creating dependable marriage partners for the African American wives.

Paradoxically, these messiahs are advocating schools for Negro boys. These schools will shield the boys from the smothering of the Great Black Mother, which suffocates their ego and the external environments, which give the black male distorted self-images and negative attitudes toward their roots. In addition to the Humanities, Math, Science, and Technology, the curriculum of these schools will include reading of autobiographies and biographies of the African and the American African heroes. They will study African religions and philosophy, African psychology, and African culture. They will have daily physical and mental exercises. Mental exercise will include debate, discussion, and friendly confrontation. They will be trained on how to turn a deaf ear to negative propaganda against African descent. They will be trained how to discard gossip, damaging allegations, witch-hunting of African American religious and political leaders.

They will be enticed to look at Africa as their Jerusalem, Garden of Eden, and cosmic center. They will be tutored on human relationship, how to relate with women, home and family life, how to build and abide in the father's house (Thingira) in order to offer protection and security to the African American mothers. They will indeed become a great asset to the Negro mother and her children.

These "seven thousand African American fathers" have discovered that they are mighty eagles with strong wings and the ability to fly into the cosmos. They are enabling the African American children to discover and use their strong wings. They are training them how to use their strong wings for flying to the world of freedom and prosperity. They are imbuing their spirits with self-determination. They give them the water of life, which is filling their lives with vitality and ability to make their own choices. They are preparing young men and women for responsible parenthood.

Back to Africa. The borrowed, unsuccessful, Western, political, and economic systems, which are superimposed on the African continent, are affecting the personality of the African father. The African father is expected to be a breadwinner. The fathers who are unsuccessful in winning the bread are also losing their egos. Some of these fathers who are living with their families are retreating to drug and alcohol dependence. They go out to the pubs for drinks and return home late at night when the children are asleep and leave. for work very early in the morning before they have seen their children. This habit has led to infidelity and irresponsibility.

In reaction to this problem, some women (including Christian women) have turned to the traditional medicine man. The latter has discovered a medicine, which the former puts in her husband's drink or food. This medication is intended to make the husband docile, domesticated, and ever bound to his wife and home, but unfortunately, most men who are served with these ingredients have become both docile and mentally retarded. Some women have regretted this and gone back to the medicine man for a cure. One wife had this dialogue with a doctor."

"After taking the medicine, my husband became mentally sick and lost his job. I need a cure for his mental disability."

"I have the medicine for docility and domestication," answered the medicine man, "but I have no medicine for neutralization." The woman was angry and disappointed realizing that she will now take care of her retarded husband as one of her children. Many a husband in the areas are harbored with the fear of being served with this stuff.

However, we still have a large number of African husbands who are dedicated and committed to their families. These fathers are found both in urban and rural areas. Likewise, we do have committed and faithful mothers. The majority of these mothers and fathers are Christians. They are more cooperative and corroborative than pre-Christian African parents. They are and will be the strong backbone to the emerging generation.

Nevertheless, these committed couples are being challenged by family responsibility, particularly if both of them are professionals with full-time jobs. They are left with no time for their children. The house maids are in charge of the children.

5. House Maids

Africans have employed men and women servants since time immemorial. They hired them for domestic work, farming, and herding. They gave them separate huts, and for that reason, a servant couldn't interfere with the nuclear or extended family. While women servants were deployed for domestic work and child care, they never substituted the parents.

In contrast, the modern maids are as substitute mothers, whose duties include child care and most of the household chores. They live under the same roof with their masters. Their presence in the house and absence of the mother has resulted in infidelity, separation, and divorce. Since most of the maids are teenage girls, who have no training in child care, most of the children are abused and undernourished. Some maids have brought calamity to children and strife in marriage. A few husbands have divorced their wives and married their maids.

In one seminar, there was a heated debate on the quality and personality type of a maid that the couples should employ. A young woman, who was a school teacher said, "I advise my husband to get me the ugliest girl in the village. This solves the problem of infidelity." "There is no ugly woman in the dark," a man with a seductive smile interjected. This man was supported by a middle-aged woman, who was an ex-house servant. We burst into laughter as she narrated her experience.

"I am a very ugly woman, who had been employed as a maid by people from varied social strata—wealthy business men, medical doctors, and university professors. None of these men have not seduced me. The worst of them all was a professor, who constantly persuaded me to go out with him to a movie. But I categorically refused. He enticed me with a lot of money, but I never yielded. Though I am a woman of the lowest class and very ugly, the professional husbands didn't mind. But I stood firm because I had Christ. So, the answer to this problem is not ugliness but Christ."

While Christ is the answer to sexual morality, it is simplistic to suggest that he is the answer to the division of labor as it relates to the maid-wife-husband triangle. The ugly maid is not an answer, either. She is but an ugly substitute mother who will develop a child with ego deflation or poor self-image. With threatening inflation and worsening economy, it is unrealistic to expect a career woman to stay at home to take care of the children. As we have seen, African mothers were not confined in the kitchen and domestic work. They fully participated in agricultural, commercial and religious duties. As with the case of Wangu wa Makeri, the women were warriors and judges.

But the modern technological and professional society demands a system that would give professional care to the children. We need daycares, which run from 6:00 a.m. to 6:00 p.m. These daycares should employ mature men and women who have done some studying in child psychology. The working parent should take their children to the daycare in the morning as they go to work and pick them up in the evening after work. While mothers should remain masters of domestic work and child's care, men should learn how to assist and fill-in. They should fight a mythological demon, which maintains that it is only a mother who can both nurse a baby and change diapers. These rituals bind the baby to the father and may save a baby boy from being homophobic. But more importantly, the mother and the father will share the duties that are performed by the maid. They will be free from the presence of an outsider who invades their privacy, and disrupts their marriage, and abuses their children. Involvement of both parents in house chores and rearing of children will develop a healthy Great Mother and Great Father in the offspring's personality. More about this on the chapters on Great Mother and Great Father.

In career choices, however, we must go beyond traditional African philosophy of division of labor. We will need illumination of the modern psychology. According to analytical psychology and Myers-Briggs personality typing, there are women who can adequately perform the duties that the ancient man attributed to males, and males who can do better duties that were ascribed to women. There are women, who like Wangu, can be able judges political and religious leaders. In this section, you have a blessing of learning how to identify your types and other types. You will then fall in love with yourself and others. After enjoying what you are and being what you are you will let others be without trying to form them in your own image.

B. PSYCHOLOGY AND DIVISION OF LABOR

IMMEDIATELY FOLLOWING MY MATRICULATION AT the School of Theology at the University of the South in the Summer of 1976, I was told that we had to do a psychological test. At that time, I had a real problem of finding places, and for that reason, I was ten minutes late for the test because I couldn't find where the class was. I was poor in observation and getting the details of the landmarks, since I was pre-occupied with intuition, I was always thinking about something, developing an idea rather than watching my direction. I was more interested in the inner world more than the outer world. I focused more to the horizon than to where I was stepping. More often than not, I had to stumble on

The Fruitful Family

something as I walked. So, even though we had been shown where the class was during the orientation, it took me time to figure out where the examination was located.

After finding the class, I was very nervous and feeling guilty for being late. I hated and still hate being late. The professor handed over to me a paper, which appeared to me as if it had five hundred questions. I answered all the questions. but I was apprehensive about the whole business of psychoanalysis. After the test, I refused to go to check out my type. I contended that there is no human laboratory which is scientific enough to analyze human beings since personality is as complex as life itself. I stayed at the University of the South for three years without checking my type. I associated type-matching with Analytical Psychology, which I disliked at the time, because everybody at the seminary was talking about C. G. Jung.

After finishing the Master of Divinity program, my wife and I audited a class on Jung under Professor Craig Anderson, who was my professor of pastoral psychology. I took the class, not because I was interested in Jung, but for my admiration of Craig. Mysteriously, anything that Craig recommended, I took it without reservation. My book shelves were full of books recommended by him. I never understood why I identified with him so much, even though he had almost no personal contact with me. On one occasion he was confronted by the students for giving them too much work. To my surprise, I felt as though it was I who was being attacked.

Professor Anderson asked the class to take the Myers Briggs Type Indicator Test. Since I could not say no to him, I cooperated. It turned out that I was an INTJ. Craig, my favorite professor, was also an INTJ. My dear wife was an ISFJ. Since that period, I developed an interest in C. G. Jung and the Myers-Briggs Type Indicator. Although Myers Briggs psychology is not scientific enough to explain the mystery of human personality, it is the best tool for helping us to know what we can do better and how our gathering and processing of data is influenced by our preferences and temperaments.

In the 1950s, Katheryn Briggs, with her daughter, Isabel Myers, illuminated by C. G. Jung's work on "psychological types," observed that there are sixteen personality types. Each of these types prefers particular patterns of action and approaches to life in his/her own way. Because of the varied temperaments and preferences, each type possesses his/her own mode of life, ways of interacting with people, and has the potential for specific duties. The differences in behavior are the results of preferences, which emerge early in life.

According to Myers-Briggs, there are four pairs of contrasting preferences. These are: Extroversion(E) vs. Introversion(I), Sensing(S) vs. Intuition(N), Thinking(T) vs. Feeling(F), Judging(J) vs. Perceiving(P). Each person develops four of the preferences while the other four remain less developed. One operates on all preferences, but the preferred preferences are as naturally employed just as the right-handed person uses the right hand more naturally than the left hand. The variation in combinations of the preferences result to sixteen personality types. These are: ISTJ, ISFJ, INFJ, INTJ, ISTP, ISFP, INFP, INTP, ESTP, ESFP, ENFP, ENTP, ESTJ, ESFJ, ENFJ, ENTJ.[11] Each of these types plays a particular role better than the other and has also some aspects that are inferior to other types. Although society tends to prefer and even reward some types more than others, none of the types are more useful than others. If an organization lacks one of the types, it tends to have some defects. Thus, all types are of equal value in the scheme of the division of labor. More about this in my book: *INITIATION AND PASTORAL PSYCHOLOGY*

C. DIVISION OF LABOR AND COUNSELING

For the counselor to be effective, the counselor should be aware of the fact that while the client's perception and interpretation of meaning is influenced by over-arching province of meaning of his country, he is also influenced by the symbolic universe of meaning of his particular people. He or she is a part of his village. Individuals and society do not denote separate phenomenon; they are, indeed, simply a collective and distributive aspect of the same. An individual is bound into the whole of which he is a member, and to consider him apart from the whole is quite as artificial as to consider society apart from individuals. As we have seen, the scriptures and African ontology delineates a human person as both and at the same time "I" and "We." Anthropos was created by "Let us"—the deity who manifested himself in oneness. Likewise, the Africans perceive an individual as both one and many. In Professor John Mbiti's words, "I am because we are, and since we are, therefore, I am."

In counseling, we must pay attention to objective psyche by examining the dreams of and studying the literature about our client. We must struggle to understand both primary and secondary groups of the individual's concern. We also ought to understand the blessings and curses of the individual's nuclear and extended family. The individuals never escape from what they have learned at home as children.

In family counseling, we need to find out whether every member of the family is playing his role or whether house chores are left in the hands of the father, mother, or maid. Are children being trained in holding family and communal responsibilities? When should training for work start? It should start in infancy. Indeed, the human should be made aware of and be trained for religious, social, political, and economical duties. Traditionally, the African parent trained the child to reciprocate by giving her the milk then the parent would sip some milk. This is done repeatedly until the child learns to volunteer to feed the mother or father. In the same manner, the mother puts food on the plate and then takes back a small portion. Gradually, the child learns how to share and to do for others what is done for him.

My wife and I commenced training for religious, political, and communal responsibilities at zero year with our children. We believe the parent should train and facilitate a child to "increase in wisdom and in stature and in favor with God and man." We guided them to wisdom by imparting our morals and ethics, which draw from

African and Judeo-Christian heritages. We trained them to take care of their bodies, which are the temple of God. We facilitated the growth in "favor with God" by instructing them in the word of God and training them to pray and to be in a worshipping community. They learned how to say their prayers when still in their cribs. We aided them in increasing in "favor with man" by our love of and respect to the people around us. We communicated to them our philosophy of humanity. We believe that while there is evil in the world, humans are fundamentally good. Their goodness is not determined by their color, race, or language. We teach them to be servants of God and human beings. Mom and Dad, and sister and brother, are a part of these invaluable communities. Thus, our children had to start by performing domestic chores. They started by doing to the parents as the parents did to them. After our toddler, Isaac Cyprian, learned how to bottle feed mom and dad at zero year, he enjoyed washing their faces in the same manner, as they do to him. On one evening, I had a startling experience. I was dozing off on the sofa after a busy day.

I was surprised by Cyprian, with a wet towel on my face. The toddler was wiping my face with a towel, which he had dipped in a toilet bowl. He was doing the best he could for the dad. Since dad wipes his face when it is dirty, he has to wipe his to keep him clean and alert.

As far as the division of labor is concerned, each member of the quartet has a specific role. The two-year-old boy turns off the TV set during the family prayer. He pulls off dad's and mom's shoes and puts them in the closet. Rehema (fifteen) is a dishwasher and assists mom in the laundry and kitchen. Mom is responsible for the kitchen, laundry, and the toddler. Dad is a garbage and yard man. We work in the garden together, buy grocery together, and have family and church worship together.

As far as temperament is concerned, each member makes a unique contribution. Mom, being an ISFJ, helps the family to project the best public image and maintains fundamental values, which we have acquired from our Kenyan-Judeo-Christian heritages. She is

The Fruitful Family

responsible for details. With her talent of remembering our past, she uses her memory to inspire our today. Our daughter, who is an ESFP, imbues the family with laughs and light-heartedness, reminding us of our anniversaries, birthdays, special days, and the importance of living and enjoying our here and now. While I am the breadwinner, Mary and Rehema are people winners. They are good at making and keeping friends.

Dad, being an INTJ, is responsible for setting the family goals and challenging the family to engage in constant self-improvement. While our varied temperaments are complimentary, they are also sources of our conflicts. For instance, while Mary and Rehema regard a particular success as an end to itself, for me it is a process to the endless end. And, thus, I have the annoying habit of making this comment, "What you have done will help you to become...." To this, sometimes, Mary and Rehema may respond in unison. "To become! Can't you be contented with what I/we have done?" Mary may irritate us with historical citations, particularly, when she uses our past so as to control our present or make us feel guilty. To this, Rehema and dad may shout antiphonically, "We cannot dwell in the past!" Rehema's personality, which is dominated by the "here and now" and "all thine is mine, and mine is thine," may prefer to have a good time first, and then work later. Mary and I may shout at her, "Work first!" She may turn this into a joke and say, "If you ever trace your roots you will discover that you are a brother and a sister." She, however, believes that our family is one of the best families in the world. Isaac Cyprian has not yet done his psychological test. But he is a clown, who enjoys tickling and being tickled. But when he was two years old, he enjoyed washing dishes with him mom. And now twenty-two year later, he is a senior chef. Ray enjoyed travel greatly. Whenever we reached our destination, her first question was: "where do we go after this. She repeated this so much that I nicknamed her Traveler. Today she is a flight attendant. She travel all over united stated. We, of course, enjoyed each other immensely, as we move from form to formless, from cosmos to chaos, and structure to antistructure. Our anti or non-structured selves are like the joints that bind us together. It is like our night, which gives us enormous appreciation of our day light.

Recently Mary and I enjoyed five days' vacation at our nephew Habel. He greatly appreciated the vision of labor in this family of four-parents and two boys-Chris and BA. Ann concentrate on home. She does her work at home. She prepare the boys for school While Habel teaches in the University and work on the yard. They boys help their mom with washing dishes and another house chore. The ten-year-old has a great passion for baking. She visit YouTube to learn all types of backing. He does banking better than his mom. Since from School the school bus takes one hour; Chris complete his homework before reaching home so as to have time for helping his mom in the kitchen. The family also attend the church regularly.

Thus, while the division of labor expresses our structured self, it is important that we understand that we have a sphere, which is antistructure, irrational, and chaotic. Hence, a complete order is impossible, and for that reason, we have a famous expression, "To err is human; to forgive is divine."

CHAPTER 16

THE ANTISTRUCTURE-NARARANJA

WHAT IS MARARANJA?

I have mentioned that irua started with mararanja dances, and that during this occasion, people were free to dance the whole night and to sleep away from the houses. I have noted that mararanja was marked with freedom of expression and freedom of being. A person was free to utter whatever was in his mind and to be whatever he liked, provided that he did not harm anyone. A person was free to be as crazy as he liked and whatever he did or said was allowed to go with the wind. Mararanja allowed people to be disorientated and antistructure.

It is my contention that mararanja externalized and ritualized a motif that is inherent not only in the Kikuyu community, but also in all human communities. Indeed, mararanja is that part of us which yearns to be away from the house—the house being an archetype of self. It is our disorientated, antistructure, and chaotic self.

Dr. John Githiga

MARARANJA AND THE INTERNATIONAL COMMUNITY

I HAVE OBSERVED MARARANJA IN international gatherings consisting of American, European, and African peoples. The most interesting international mararanja in which I have participated was during the staff institute of the Association of Theological Institutions in Eastern Africa (ATIEA). The gathering included American, German, British, and African religious educators. Mararanja occurred when we were holding a farewell party for one of the members of staff who was nicknamed "Uncle David." The whole party was marked with excessive freedom of expression. We played "the child" and became antistructure. The Bible was read in an awkward and heretical way. The reader started reading from the last word of the last sentence of the last paragraph of the last chapter of the last book of the Old Testament. History was also taught backwards. The whole occasion was marked with a feeling of joy and liberation. Just as the initiates became everything, they were not supposed to be during mararanja, we became everything that a good teacher ought not to be.

Furthermore, I witnessed several mararanja when I was studying in the United States. I was astonished to observe mararanja that were very similar to the Kikuyu ones. These ceremonies were cyclical. They occurred during the orientation program for the new students and the last supper for the senior students.

The orientation ceremonies included cookouts, putting on masks, "playing the fool," and excessive freedom of expression. During the farewell party for the senior students, the middle students dramatized the idiosyncrasies of the senior students and faculty members. The mannerisms of the professors and the leaving students were so exaggerated that some professors became angry and decided never to attend senior's farewell parties again.

The integration of the sexes is one of the answers. Let the boys and the girl's study together, confront and compete with each other and become familiar with one another and learn how to live together as sexual beings. As was traditional, young men and

The Fruitful Family

women who were initiated together, and lived in the same lodge and attended the same school, these students were in an integrated school learning how to live together like an age group. The girls ceased to appear beautiful, but weak angels in the eyes of boys. They became real human beings with their strengths and short comings. They ceased to be mere sexual objects by demonstrating that their psychic energy was equal to that of the boys. On the other hand, the girls will discover that boys are not all-powerful protecting angels, but human beings with strengths and weaknesses. They learn the psychology of how to handle the persons of the opposite sex. By sitting together in the class, playing together and rubbing each other's shoulders, they learn how to experience their sexuality without coitus or what the Bible terms as fornication. Christian unions that allow both young men and women to be together, to praise God at the top of their voices, and just become ecstatic can provide an outlet for their irrationality. It is in this respect that Christian unions, and charismatic movements are useful for youths.

The school, college, and university can minimize or even prevent abnormal communal lostness by organizing social evenings, which include students and teachers. This should provide a complete freedom of expression. All should be free to operate through the mararanja sphere. Since mararanja is both non-structured and antistructure, the teachers ought to be vulnerable enough for negative criticism. But whatever is said at this time should be allowed to go with the wind.

In St. Paul's United Theological College, we played our mararanja during social evenings and what we called "teach-ins" and college fellowships. During the teach-in, all the students and tutors gathered to debate a particular motion. In addition to being rational, one is free to be irrational and express ones' feelings in ones' own way. One is also free to confront. The students confront each other. They also confront the tutors and the college authority. The tutors also enjoy confronting each other and the college authority.

The college fellowship brings the students, tutors and the members of the College Council together. We confront each other. The students and the tutors express their feelings about the members of the College Council—and the authority figures. On the other hand, the members of the council may challenge and confront the students and the tutorial staff. In most cases, the members of the council find it very rough since they do not expect attack and irrational expression from the scholars. Consequently, some of them do not attend the fellowship. One of the council members who decided never to attend the fellowship was reported to have said, "If fellowship means confrontation, I shall never attend it again." However, a good number of the members of the council, allowing themselves to be vulnerable, have continued to attend this annual fellowship. On this occasion, our mararanja is given freedom to express itself. We normally have five hours of mutual confrontation and attack. This is followed by the service of the word of God and Holy Communion. Consequently, the college community is left with great love, peace, and unity. This saves us from abnormal lostness.

In addition, the social evening brings the whole college community together. The program includes concerts, roleplays, jesting, and laughter. The students enjoy the freedom, over exaggerating the traits of teachers and the college authority. This occasion provides an excessive freedom of expression.

This type of get-together, which brings the students, teachers, and administration together, can save the institution from abnormal lostness, such as ceaseless crying, laughing, or strikes that could result in destroying the college ideals. Nevertheless, it has to be born in mind that lostness is a motif that is in both an individual and a community. Thus, at times we have to be mixed up or as we say in Kiswahili, "tutachanganyikiwa." We have, therefore, to go through a period of alienation, precariousness, and disorientation. Yet, this is the time when we must be on our guard since the devil will exploit the state of lostness to take us to captivity. We must pray without ceasing as our Lord Jesus Christ did. We must be in him who is the Way.

The Fruitful Family

As we have seen, we get lost during the rites of passage when we are moving from one developmental stage to another, from one social status to another, from one place to another. We are also affected by the passages of our loved ones. We may become temporarily disoriented during the death of our parent, our child, our brother, or our sister. This lostness, whether normal or abnormal, is not without pain.

CHAPTER 17

THE STRUCTURE

A. THE STRUCTURE

While precircumcision dances gave the initiates an unlimited freedom of expression and of being unstructured, the dances prepared them for the actual day of operation, when they were expected to be totally structured. They were expected to control their feelings, emotions, and bodily expressions. At the peak of pain, they were expected to sit or stand still like stones. Mugo Gacheru narrates how he felt during his highest point of pain. "He (the circumciser) held my penis, pulled the foreskin, and cut it. It was very, very, painful. But I did not show any feeling of fear or even acted as if I were being cut. No medical aid was applied first or later, and this made it extremely painful." Although Gacheru felt a lot of pain, he was expected to sit emotionless. This was a symbolic expression of the life of an initiated person. He was expected to be well behaved and organized. As a Kikuyu proverb put it: "Thiga is circumcised, there is no more mararanja." This means we are not at a mararanja occasion and, therefore, we must be intentional and rational. Whatever one says, he will be accountable for it. Thus, while the initiated person was free to release his sphere, which is mararanja once every year during mararanja and occasionally with his age-group, he was expected to be well mannered, to respect and obey those in authority and to live in accordance with social norms. As we have seen, the kikuyu community was well organized. Each one knew what to do and what was expected of him. Here we can move from particular to universal and argue that structure is found in every human community. All people have norms and laws that govern them. There is no country that has automobiles and no traffic laws. The drivers know whether they have to drive on the right or left sides. So, when driving, we are expected to be structured, rational and intentional. Indeed, we are expected to respect and obey the law. The structured sphere in us enables us to do so.

B THE STRUCTURE AND RELIGION

IT IS VERY INTERESTING TO note that Paul discusses the structured spheres of human personality within the context of life in the spirit (Roman 7:12, 14; 1 Corinthians 12–14). He termed this sphere law, order, and mind. He saw it as holy, just, good, and spiritual. He advised the Church to use this sphere in intergroup relations, teaching, preaching, liturgy, and public speech. In these passages, Paul saw the tension between antistructure and the structured self. He admonished his readers to use mararanja in their private prayers or in a group in which all the members have undergone the same experience. However, in their relations with the outsiders, they should be rational, intentional, and structured. "For if the whole church assembles and all speak in tongues, and the outsiders or unbelievers enter, will they not say that you are mad," Paul indicated to his readers that God has given them power to control their mararanja, "For God is not a God of confusion but of peace." He reminds them that "the spirits of prophets are subject to prophets."

In the history of Christian thought, Richard Hooker is one of the thinkers who advocated the structured sphere. Like Paul, he used the term "law" to describe this entity. He put law under two categories: the first law eternal and the second law eternal. Through the first law eternal, God governs himself by his own voluntary act. He governs the natural agents, celestial beings, and national creatures. In other words, for Hooker, rationality or reason is divine, supernatural, rational, scriptural, and human. Of course, Hooker himself lived a very structured life. As one historian wrote, "His voice was low, stature little, gesture none at all, standing stone-still in the pulpit, as if the posture of his body were the emblem of his mind, unmovable in his opinions." Possibly owing to the strong opposition from Puritans who were against the law and structure, Hooker took an extreme position and suppressed his mararanja. However, he reminds us that we cannot live without law and order. As we shall see later, law and order, rationality and intentionality, are some of the attributes of the Great Father.

C. THE ANTISTRUCTURE AND STRUCTURE

To this end, it suffices to say that we need to balance between the antistructure self and structured self. We should know where and when to be structured. For instance, we cannot avoid being structured in our daily work, when driving, in the law court, and when we are interacting with strangers. We should have the freedom of living our antistructure self during mararanja (e.g., the eve of All Saints Day, the Feast of the Fools, the ceremonies of separation, social evenings, and when we are with our cliques, age groups, and primary groups. It would also be rewarding if we could have a day once in a while when one can walk at random. At this time, we need to listen to and obey our day dreams and fantasies. This would be a celebration of our mararanja or irrationality. Rank identified the vitality and dynamism of the spheres.

The Fruitful Family

He advised his readers to release and accept them.

The only remedy is an acceptance of the fundamental irrationality of the human being and life in general, an acceptance which means not merely a recognition or even admittance of our basic primitivity in the sophisticated vein of our typical intellectuals, but a real allowance for its dynamic functioning in human behavior, which would not be lifelike without it." For Rank, real life meant expression of both the rational and irrational self. Here one can conclude that if the inner mararanja is totally buried, this results in violence and neurosis. The situation can even worsen during the "passages" and lead to an abnormal lostness.

CHAPTER 18

LOSTNESS

A. WHAT IS LOSTNESS

The word lostness is used with a notion of temporary confusion, conflict, disorientation, and precariousness, which one undergoes during the rites of passage. It includes the idea of a Swahili word, "kuchanganyikiwa," being mixed up. It also bears the meaning of a Kikuyu word, "Guturura," meaning a temporary blindness, which one experiences when one is dazzled, or lost for a while. A person undergoes lostness when he is confronted with choices. For example, when one is in a situation whereby there are so many open doors, yet one must enter through one of them; or when one hears so many conflicting voices, yet must listen and follow only one of them. So lostness refers to the state of mind before one makes a choice.

As we have seen, the genius of the irua lies in the fact that the entire community celebrated, ritualized, and externalized the inner lostness of adolescence. This ritualization was performed during the mararanja dances when the community became ecstatic, disorientated, and non-structured. It is my thesis that what was externalized during this occasion is a reality that is inherent in every individual and every human community. We undergo a state of temporary confusion or disorientation when we are moving from one developmental stage to another, from one place to another, and from one social status to another. This lostness can be either individual (that is, affecting one person) or communal (that is, affecting a group of people).

B. COMMUNAL LOSTNESS

LET ME ILLUSTRATE WHAT I mean by communal lostness. I have just delivered a lecture on the "stages of development from birth to old age" to the Family Life Education, and in-service course for Kenya school teachers held at Limuru Conference Centre. After the delivery, the teachers asked far reaching questions about the problems that are facing the youth. One of these questions was about a communal lostness. The question was: *What is the cause of the recurrent hysteria that sweeps across East African girls' boarding secondary schools?* Normally, this phenomenon sparks from one school and then spreads to other schools. Its nature is that one girl starts laughing or crying then eventually all the girls cry. Gradually, this uncontrollable emotional outburst sweeps across girls' boarding schools in East Africa. In some schools, this lostness is so severe that it results in a temporary closure of the school. Dr. Sebastian K. Lutahoire writes that these were not isolated cases of "examination fever." For instance, sometimes whole schools had to be closed because of mass hysteria, a state of mental disturbance. One of the Christian girls' schools in West Lake Region, Tanzania had to close for this reason for a period of time. 1

In a different form, this communal lostness is evident in our colleges and universities. The students may boycott the lectures, become unruly, and throw stones at passers-by. This may lead to a temporary closure of the institution.

Dr. John Githiga

In Africa, where people unite behind a person rather than a system, the whole county may be left stranded when the head of the state dies or when he is over-thrown. In Kenya, for instance, the whole country was left stranded when the death of the late Mzee Jomo Kenyatta was announced. The majority of the Kenyans were hysterical and did not know what to do and where to go. They were temporarily confused.

More often than not, the church experiences communal lostness when she is moving from one era to another or when she is ushering in a new orthodoxy. She had a real struggle when she was admitting the first generation of gentile Christians. This trend continued in all epochs of the history of the church and will never halt until Christ comes.

The most recent incident that sparked off the debate in the Anglican communion is the election and consecration of Barbara Harris as suffrican bishop of Massachusetts. The consecration was a rite of passage for both Bishop Harris and Catholic Christendom, which claims unbroken apostolic succession of the episcopate. This single event, which took place in Massachusetts, had and will continue to have enormous effect on the Anglican communion and the Roman Catholic and protestant churches.

For the innovators, liberals, and radicals, the inclusion of women in the episcopate was hailed. It was perceived as a glimmer of light and an act of obedience to the creator God who commanded, "Let there be light." In the words of Rev. Paul Washington, the preacher at consecration service, "The light which we see today began its journey before the beginning of time." To most Christians to have a woman bishop was an indication of church growth in equality and inclusiveness. For that very reason, the majority of the people who attended the historic event were hopeful, proud, and happy. While the celebration was a sacred carnival to the innovators, liberals, and radicals, it was a sacrilegious imposture to the traditionalists. They saw it as an insult to the church. It was contrary to the established orthodoxy—the scriptures, tradition, and constitution of the Episcopal Church. Some people in this camp regarded consecration of a woman bishop as a death. One rector symbolized this feeling by holding a requiem mass. He contended, "I just thought that it is good time to pray for the dead and the dying, and that includes the Diocese of Massachusetts."

Ironically, the consecration of a woman bishop was a matter of death and life. It marked a death of an era in which the highest order in Christendom was a "man's society." It was also a birth of an era of total inclusion of male and female in all hierarchies of the church. As the presiding bishop rightly put it, it was "a gift to the Catholic Church and a contribution toward a deeper understanding of the holy orders."

The point that I am making is that the church as a body of Christ experienced substantial conflict during her transitional period. This does not mean that the entire body is disoriented. But some members may be confused and secede from the main fellowship.

C. THE POSITIVITY AND NEGATIVITY OF LOSTNESS

AS I HAVE POINTED OUT, individual lostness may occur when one is moving from one developmental stage to another, such as adolescence, young adulthood, mature adulthood, and old age. This state of mind may be experienced when one attains a particular rank in church or in society. For example, a person may be temporarily confused immediately after being consecrated a bishop. One may experience a similar feeling after achieving a particular academic qualification. I remember how I felt when I received a letter stating that I had fulfilled all the requirements for a doctoral degree. I was so excited and could not do anything for a week. I felt like a new driver who had just passed his driving test and had been so used to driving with a co-driver, but now had to drive alone.

Lostness may lead to either a negative or a positive result. It may, for instance, lead an adolescent to either delinquency, or joining a charismatic group. The lostness of the mid-life may result in divorce, taking a second wife, deserting the family, joining a seminary, going back to school, or to an excessive search for material things. Lostness during retirement may result in destroying that which the person has built, and bitterness against the emerging authority figures. When the man in authority is approaching the retirement age, he may project his retirement to his subordinates and force them to retire. The head of the state, for instance, may imprison or even eliminate the best politicians who are likely to succeed him. Similarly, a bishop who is about to retire may persecute his priests, particularly those who have potentials for episcopate. I know of a bishop, who when he was approaching the extreme age and his retirement, started giving his priests a hard time. He used constant and unrealistic transfers as a punishment. One priest, who had children in school, was forced to move to another parish within forty-eight hours. He waged war with those priests who were possible candidates for succeeding him. He bragged that he was using better strategy than Adolph Hitler, who foolishly fought several countries together and, therefore, lost the battle. The bishop's strategy was to fight one priest at a time.

In the morning and the early afternoon of his life, this bishop was a facilitator and enabler of the priests. He was a model priest whose parish had produced more priests than any other parish in the diocese. Yet in the twilight of his life, he became disoriented. He abandoned all the ideals that he had cherished in the morning. He became, as it were, a sun that was contradicting itself. The sun drew its rays instead of emitting them. Its light and warmth were declining and being extinguished. Said differently, he became a dry well. The valley which had streams of water in the morning had dried up in the late afternoon. The fertile crescent became barren in the autumn of life.

If home and school life have not provided proper guidance, an individual may lose himself, even in the morning of his life, in such a way that he will not come to himself again. The person may be used to taking drugs and become totally addicted to them. He may become a life-long alcoholic. This misguided individual may deviate from social norms and become delinquent, criminal, and irreligious.

On the other hand, the period of lostness may be a time of great learning and personality growth. For instance, a young person who joins a charismatic or revival movement may gain a spirituality, which he will never lose. A middle-aged person who goes back to school may attain an immense spiritual and intellectual growth. A person who is led by his lostness to a far country, like the prodigal son, may learn how to appreciate his country and his father's house. Like the prodigal son, I celebrated my mid-life lostness in a far country—America. This for me was a time of enormous learning. Being free from the demons and taboos of my father's house, I had the opportunity to learn a great deal about human nature and life in general. I had the privilege of looking objectively at my country and, therefore, becoming aware of our cultural strengths and weaknesses. I distinguished between that which is uniquely African from that which is human. Aside from learning how to accept and appreciate people of other cultures, I had a fresh interest in "my father's house." By being bi-cultural, I became freer with others and with myself.

A person who is undergoing lostness should neither be segregated nor excommunicated. He or she needs to be accepted, appreciated, and loved. In counseling, this person needs to be directed to the Great Father, the Great Mother, and the Tree of God. As we shall see later, a healthy personality is that which balances among and draws life from the three archetypes. A male who has a sick masculine component (animus) finds it difficult to face the Great Father. A woman who suppresses her femininity and a man who has an unhealthy feminine component (anima) will have a problem with the Great Mother. A person with a sick religion does not like to approach the Tree of God. (More about this in Chapters Thirteen, Fourteen, and Fifteen.)

D. THE CAUSES AND TREATMENT OF LOSTNESS

How do we go about the communal confusion? First of all, we need to know the cause of this behavior. Among other things, there are physiological, physiological, social, and religious causes. As we have seen in Chapter Four, physiologically, the adolescents are bothered by the increase of height and weight, by being too short or too tall, by motor awkwardness, by the growth of the primary and secondary sexual organs, and the unevenness of the rate of sexual maturation for both sexes. Psychologically, they go through a turmoil caused by the infantile repressed urges. These feelings are intensified; thus, the previous defenses are no longer adequate, and therefore a sweeping readjustment is required. Psychosocially, the adolescent mind is in a flux. This is a psycho-social stage between child morality and the ethics to be developed by the adult. Socially, they experience tension between home and school norms and the expectation of the peer group. Religiously, adolescents may experience conflict between their parents' teaching and what they learn from the media and their peer group.

If the school authorities and the parents could be aware of the above facts, this could partly solve the problems of an abnormal lostness. They would not do this by segregating the girls from boys and applying rigid puritanical rules.

I was privileged to visit a girls' school a few days after the communal lostness. The school was managed and sponsored by the Roman Catholics. All the teachers in the school were nuns and all the students were girls. No male could enter the school compound without special permission. The girls were not allowed to leave the school without being accompanied by a nun. One of the incidents that triggered the lostness was the case of a girl who broke the regulation and went to the town for shopping without the presence of a female teacher. Coming back in the evening, the girl was expelled from school. Since her home was six hundred kilometers away from the school, the girl had to wander about at night looking for accommodation. Luckily, she managed to find an Anglican priest's family who accommodated her and gave her food. This incident was followed by an outbreak of laughter. All the girls laughed and laughed and nobody was able to halt their laughter.

Some of them continued laughing for so long a time that they had to be taken to the hospital.

It is not impossible to discern the cause of this peculiar lostness. Since this type of hysteria does not occur in day secondary schools or boarding schools, which include both sexes, we could deduce that one of the causes is sex segregation. These females are kept away from the males when they need them most. They are asexualized when their sexuality has reached its zenith. They are compelled to repress the libido when all their defense mechanisms are incapable of doing so. This is just like stopping up all the outlets of a cooking pot when the food is boiling, or like preventing a child from disease infection by sealing his nose and mouth so that he may not inhale the polluted air.

Another cause of this lostness could be a contradiction between the teachers' culture that was enforced to the girls and the girls' traditional culture, which dominated their consciousness, personal unconscious, and objective psyche. In school, the students were indoctrinated with missionaries' culture while the home trained them to live and grow like African women. Dr. B. Kagwa did a clinical study of the communal lostness, which occurred in the Christian girls' schools in West Lake Region, Tanzania. He concluded that this phenomenon was caused by the difficult situation for the young people. For at school and churches, they were indoctrinated with new beliefs; at home, they were exposed to traditions. This contrast must be resolved in one way or another. To eliminate the anxiety, one may choose between "going native" or reverting to total westernization. As in these epidemics, one may elect to get sick to escape difficult situations.

This bears a lot of truth about students' conflicts. In school, they are introduced to a male less community; at home, they live in a community of males and females and are trained to grow as heterosexual human beings. The missionary school segregates them according to their sexes, traditional school is sexually integrated. In school they are taught to believe and adhere to an asexualized deity, at home this deity is irrelevant. So, these conflicts put young people into a difficult situation. They become confused.

Another cause of this emotional outbreak is the denial and suppression of the mararanja. As we have seen, this is the human sphere that is anti-structured, non-structured, and irrational. Since this sphere is real, creative, and forceful, it can strongly steam out or dynamically react like a storm if it is totally suppressed. If this happens in school, this dynamic reaction is beyond the control of both the students and the teachers.

How can we save the students, from abnormal communal lostness, which results in either a group hysteria or school strike? How can we allow the spirit to move on this formless and chaotic sphere and therefore continue the creation of order, form, and unity?

CHAPTER 19

PAIN

A. THE PARTICULARITY AND UNIVERSALITY OF PAIN

As we have seen, the initiates were expected to confront pain with courage. During the actual operation, which was very painful, they sat or stood still, without showing bodily movement or any emotion. This was an act of ritualization of pain, which is inherent in the human life cycle. Pain is real in every human community. As one writer has said, "Walk slowly for everyone you meet has a cross." Let me illustrate this with an experience from the staff institute of the Association of Theological Institutions of Eastern Africa, which was held in Arusha, Tanzania in April, 1982.

The Institute included religious educators from Sudan, Uganda, Kenya, Tanzania, and Ethiopia who belonged to Roman Catholic, Anglican, and Protestant Churches. Being drawn from several African states, the United States of America, and European countries, the members belonged to various political ideologies. In addition, they had differing theological convictions since they operated from various theological models. This of course included orthodox, neo-orthodox liberal, radical, and revisionist models. The theme of the Arusha Institute was "Pre-Christian theologies and their implication in Christian theologies."

The topics dealt with included "Concepts of Revelation in Christianity," "Concepts of God in Africa," "Concepts of God in Christianity," "Concepts of Salvation in Africa," "Concepts of Salvation and Christianity," "Religion and Society in Africa," and "Religion and Society in Christianity." The papers dealing with each of the above topics were presented. All the papers, according to my assessment, were of the highest theological and philosophical qualities. Every presenter had done his "homework." However, each of the presentations was followed by strong arguments and disagreement. The issue was whether or not African traditional religions had full and complete salvation. Dr. Kibicho argued strongly for the full and complete saving power within African religions. This hypothesis bothered the missionaries.

The missionaries' bitter feelings toward African traditional religion were expressed by a question that was directed to Dr. Kibicho by a white teacher: "If African religion had a full and complete salvation, why did you become a Christian minister rather than a witch doctor?"

After the presentation of all the papers, the writer had to organize a forum. The majority of the participants who were put on the panel were introverted, and had no chance of saying a word for three days. The procedure was that those on the panel had to start by saying something about themselves. After this, everyone was free to ask a question, make a statement, confession, or give a testimony.

To the writer's surprise, every person started sharing his pain. Arguments and disagreements halted. Behind high quality philosophical and theological papers there was found a common ground–suffering and pain. In the majority of the states that were presented, Christians had and were still being persecuted. Thus, in pain and suffering, we were all united and had a feeling for each other. Pain is a reality. Pain is universal. C. S. Lewis rightly contend that the possibility of pain is inherent in the very existence of a world where souls can meet.

Pain may be a spiritual or mental distress—a bodily torment or a distressing sensation in a particular part of the body. Physical pain may be caused by an accident, sickness, or some chemical problems in the body. Spiritual pain may be caused by sin or keeping aloof from the religious community. Chemical disorder, an unpleasant environment, movement from one place to another and from one developmental stage to another, the attainment of anew social status, and bereavement can bring mental suffering. As Raymond Schmitt observed the amount of mental pain experienced may in part depend on the distance between one's actual state and one's ideal state. That is a gap between what one actually is and what one wishes to be.

Mental pain can be caused by a discrepancy between what a person thinks he can become and what he can actually become. For instance, one may wish to be a musician while having no potential for music.

B. PAIN AND RELIGION

AS WE HAVE SEEN, PAIN is one of the motifs in the passages of Christ. First of all, he was born in a manger. Moreover, when he was twelve, he went with his parents to Jerusalem. His parents lost him in the temple and it must have pained them to lose him for three days. Before starting his ministry, he was led by the Holy Spirit to the wilderness where he was tempted by the devil; he was hungry and thirsty. Finally, he was rejected by his own people—the chief priests, the scribes, and the elders. Consequently, he went through the agony of the cross. He was killed and buried in tomb. On the third day, God raised him from the dead and "highly exalted Him, and bestowed on him the name which is above every name" (Philippians 2:9).

Jesus understood very well that pain was a part of his life and that it was the divine plan for him to suffer. Pain and suffering was a part of his service to man and God, "for the son of man also came not to be served but to serve, and to give his life as a ransom for many" (Mark 10:45).

Paul understood Christian suffering as a participation in and identification with Christ. "If we have died with Christ, we believe that we are also to live with him" (Roman 6:5, 8). It is only by accepting the pain of the cross that a Christian will be glorified and exalted with and in Christ. For Paul, life was a struggle and victory, death and resurrection. Pain, therefore, is not a hypothesis but a reality. It can have a positive or a negative effect. It may lead to inappropriate anger, guilt, depression, or withdrawal. If a person loses a loved one, he may be bitterly angry with God or other people. He may feel guilt for not doing what he was "supposed to do." He may have a prolonged aloneness, which may lead to an extreme loneliness. He may condemn someone who is suspected to have caused the death. The bereaved may seek comfort from drugs and become alcoholic or drug addicted.

C. PAIN AND PERSONALITY GROWTH

ERIK H. ERIKSON THEORIZED THAT the pain that a person experiences during maturational stages may have a permanent negative effect on his personality. A child who lacks a reliable and dependable mother may develop basic mistrust and consequently develop the most dangerous defense mechanism—introjection and projection. In introjection, he makes other people's pain and "garbage" his own; in projection he throws his undesirable qualities and inner hurt to others. He blames others for his own evil. If the child is over-controlled, he may develop shame and doubt. Subsequently, he may become a person who tries to force the world not to look at him and to destroy the eyes of the whole world. He may blame things and regard them as evil only because they exist. He may also develop guilt and inferiority feelings. He may be feeling guilt for what he is and feel inadequate in the presence of his tool partners. He may suffer from ego-diffusion. In adulthood, one may suffer from self-absorption, stagnation, and despair. In old days in the Kikuyu community, if a person became stagnant, despairing, and totally withdrawn from the community, he was burned alive in his own house. Thus, pain may block the road to integrity and can be destructive to oneself and to others. On the other hand, pain can help an individual to attain intimacy and integrity.

Kikuyu and other African people realize that pain can make a positive contribution to one's maturation and prosperity. This is expressed by numerous expressions and proverbs. Kikuyu for instance has a proverb, which says, "Pain cannot be felt by one for the other" (Ruo rutiguanagirwo). This means that it is through suffering that one becomes an individual and attains self identity. In Kiswahili, we say, "subira huvuta heri" (patience evokes or brings blessing). This implies that it is by accepting suffering that one receives blessings from others, and being blessed, one can also bless. Ironically, acceptance of pain and suffering is seen by African people, as the key to comfort and prosperity. Our parents and teachers tell us, "patience is the key to comfort". We are advised, "follow bees and get honey". It is only by accepting the sting of the bees that you can get honey. The African believes that tribulation is followed by comfort and prosperity. It is maintained that a good omen lies beyond the obstacles, "Munyaka wi mbere ya kahinga."

According to Erik Erikson, if the child is well guided during maturational pain, he attains basic trust, autonomy, initiative, industry, and self-identity. Subsequently, when he matures, he gains intimacy, generativity, and integrity. For Erikson, integrity is the ultimate goal of a well-adjusted personality. The person who attains this goal is one who has taken care of things and people, and has adapted himself to triumphs and disappointments (pain)— someone who has been the originator of others or the generator of products and ideas. This view is at the heart of the African understanding of personality. It is maintained that integrity is the summit of personality. The individual who attains it is one who has contributed to and drawn from the community. This is expressed by proverbs such as: "He who eats alone dies alone" and "You become wise by accepting the advice of wise men." Kikuyu see a connection between wisdom and pain. One of the terms used for initiation is "The wisdom of Kikuyu." To undergo the pains and ordeals of initiation is regarded as a means of assimilating the whole gamut of tradition, norms, custom, values, and wisdom of the tribe.

D. PAIN AND PHILOSOPHY

EXISTENTIAL PHILOSOPHERS, LIKE THE TRADITIONAL men maintained that painful experiences can lead to wisdom. They witnessed a direct connection between suffering and wisdom. Their perception was influenced by the anguish, which pervaded their epoch—the horror of the two world wars, which destroyed national, regional, and cosmic centers; political and religious totalitarianism, revolutions and terrorism, slave trade, and apartheid; and spiritual bankruptcy, caused by materialism and worship of science and technology. There were also agonizing conflicts between democracy and dictatorship, individualism versus collectivism, colonization versus decolonization, freedom of thought or anti-intellectualism, and pluralistic society or absolute values and conformity. People of this era lived in tension between suppression or expression, reformation, or conformation.

Thus, influenced by their daily experiences and observations, the existentialists asserted that humans lived in distress caused by fear of nothingness and alienation. They observed that anguish is the underlying, all pervasive, universal condition of human nature. Humans live in a stormy world that is devoid of peace. They are thrown into the world against their will. As Sorem Kierkegaard lamented, "Who am I? How did I come into the world? Why was I not consulted?" Kierkegaard perceived himself as a creature who was thrown into the world against his will. He was thrown here to be there for a short duration only to be soon swallowed up in the eternity. While he was in this temporal life, he occupied a minute space and was ignorant of the rest of the universe. This situation caused mental and physical strains.

In addition, existentialists asserted that renaissance philosophers contributed to human suffering by alienating the humans from the absolute. They killed the ideal Judeo-Christian God by their empiricism, which overstressed empirical verification. This was in direct opposition to Christian principles, which advocated: "We go by faith, not by sight." By loss of belief in God, humans have lost the foundation of their truth and values.

Thus, the humans are agonized by being alienated from their traditional values and their social systems and, thereby, live lives of vanity and meaninglessness. They are estranged from the product of their labor and their religious and political systems. I witnessed this estrangement when I was a theological student at St. Paul's United Theological College. As a part of our theological studies, we had to take urban mission, which among other things, entailed spending two weeks in a factory. I was assigned to work at a textile factory in Thika. We had to stand beside the feelingless machine and operate and feed it for eight hours. The blow-room was poorly maintained and for that reason we had to inhale a lot of cotton dust. Being allergic to dust, I had a terrible cough by the end of the two weeks.

The workers who mistook me for a member of the government's special branch (plain clothed police officer), sent by the government to probe the company, shared all their problems with bitterness. One man narrated his predicament, "I left my wife and children in the countryside two years ago. Never have I gone back since. For after paying all my bills I have no money left to take to my wife. Half of my income pays the rent. A quarter is spent on my poor diet. The other portion goes to a prostitute who washes and massages my exhausted feet and soothes me to give me the comfort I need. I do not know how I will provide for my family. I am worried about them and about my old age." This worker was articulating an anguish experienced by many workers in many countries who are alienated from their families—the product of their labor, their political, social, and religious institutions.

Existentialists assert that human suffering is exasperated by the structure lessness of life. Humans live without anything to structure their beings and their world. They hover at the abyss in fear and trembling. Thrown into nothingness, they move into nothingness and will end up into nothingness—which is death. This final nothingness terminates an individual as a conscious being.

It should be borne in mind that human history by characterized by passages. These passages, according to culture-epoch theory have three phases: periods of balance, periods of chaos, and periods of adjustment. The period of balance is marked with harmony in basic institutions such as family, school, cult, and politics. Life is very satisfying particularly in the early stage of balance. Eventually, people get bored by the balance. And the new thinkers, artists, and scientists upset the balance and usher in a period of chaos.

In the period of chaos, people find themselves in the wilderness or limbo. This is analogous to mararanja in Kikuyu initiation, whereby nothing is structured. Traditional values do not hold. There are wars and civil strife. While some people strive for new balance, others will try to back the clock to a better and more peaceful "Egypt." Gradually, new discoveries and ideals are accepted. These new attitudes usher in the period of adjustment, whereby people change to conform to the new realities.

Existential philosophy was born out of the period of chaos of human civilization. It was endeavoring to give meaning to human suffering. Existentialists were asking a simple question: "What is it?" The immediate answer was, "It is painful." They then posed other questions. *What is the effect of pain on humans? What can we learn from pain?*

Some of these great thinkers discovered that there is connection between pain and moral and religious growth. Sorem Kierkegaard, for instance, observed that there are three stages of moral development: the aesthetic stage, ethical stage, and religious stage. The aesthetic stage, which is the lowest stage, is characterized by pure sensation and a life of feeling rather than thinking. People who are in this stage live in anonymity. They move with the crowd and are, as it were, in the midway of a carnival being attracted by many games and exhibits. As Plato observed, this stage is lowest in the level of understanding of reality. Persons in this stage can only know the images, reflections, and shadows rather than the real objects. They live in illusion. They are like prisoners chained in the cave, facing the opposite direction of the entrance of the cave. These prisoners can only see the shadow of the real objects.

An individual move from aesthetical to the ethical stage after a shocking experience such as an accident, serious illness, or loss of a loved one. The highest stage, which Kierkegaard terms a leap of faith or religious stage, is not only attained through painful experiences, but it also leads to greater pain and anguish. This stage is attained by a few. The best example is Abraham, who had to experience the pain of childlessness. And then when he got Isaac, the only son, whom he had yet to sacrifice. He had to murder his own son in obedience to God. As we have seen, it was ordeals and pain that the initiates experienced that made them adults. At the same token, the same pain qualified their parents to be the members of the jury.

Thus, pain, if taken positively can lead to maturity. It can set us free. And like freed prisoners, we can move from the cave to enjoy fresh air, sunshine, and beauty of creation, as well as facing the thunderstorms and hurricanes of life. We experience greater pleasure and greater pain. We discover that there is more to the cosmos than the shadows and images which we have been accustomed to in the cave. We become conscious of universal, spiritual essences. We become cognizant of dialectical realities. We accept the ambiguity of life. We become self transcendent.

Jean Paul Sartre, the father of existentialism, asserted that there is a relationship between anguish and philosophy. He contended that the consciousness of nothingness is the basis of scientific and philosophic inquiry. For Sartre, a human being is a conscious being who is made conscious by the external objects. He is a "being for-itself" which is activated by the being in-itself (all external objects, which includes other humans). Being for-itself (I, as opposed to all external objects and other humans) is empty, nothing, and transparent. There is a gap between being for-itself and being in-itself.

As conscious beings, we are agonized for being cognizant of our freedom. We dread the awareness of the fact that we are undetermined and, thus, spontaneous, and we have the power of putting a gap between our present and the past. We can make new choices, which are free, and yet it pains us to know that we are responsible for our choices. We are responsible for our perceptions and the meanings that we give to the situations in which we live. Thus, for Sartre, we have a shattering awareness that by being totally free we are also are totally responsible for our choices. This freedom brings dizziness and anguish. Anguish is therefore the outcome of freedom. For Sartre, freedom is neither a gift nor a choice. We are condemned to be free. The limit to freedom is freedom itself. We are not free to cease to be free; hence, we cannot escape from anguish which results from freedom.

On the one hand, I agree with Sartre that I am free to make choices and that I am responsible for my choices. There is also a connection between freedom and pain. As I write this chapter, my son who is eleven months has gone through two infantile developmental stages—teething and walking. Each of these stages is a movement to freedom—teething leads to freedom of chewing solid food. Yet whenever each tooth was appearing, he had a lot of discomfort. At one time, he cried one full hour. The crying was halted after smearing his gums with teething gel. After having upper and lower teeth he has acquired greater freedom of chewing, yet this freedom led to suffering since he was chewing anything that he could lay his hands on. He also had to experience pain related to the freedom of walking. In his first week of walking, he constantly hurt himself as he fell on objects that were in his way.

Thus, it is evident that freedom comes with pain and leads to pain. But on the other hand, existentialists have overstressed human suffering. Since their philosophy is a philosophy without God, they never realized the positive and salvific aspect of suffering. One of the greatest blessings of being a Christian is that a Christian experiences grace in suffering. In Paul's words, "We rejoice in our sufferings, knowing that suffering produces endurance, and endurance produces character, and character produces hope, and hope does not disappoint us, because God's love has been poured into our heart through the Holy Spirit which has been given to us" (Roman 5:3–5).

The Existentialists have missed the boat by ignoring the Being-who-let-it-be and the Being who is the ground of our being. Furthermore, their philosophy of freedom is one-legged, in that they thought that an individual could be totally free from communality. As we have seen, humans are born as "I" and "we." We are created with a capacity of being "I-ness" and "We-ness." An individual with real and healthy freedom is one who endeavors to balance between individuality and communality.

Killing of the Great Father is another weak point of existential philosophy. Sartre, for instance, never forgave his father for dying when he (Sartre) was an infant or his grandfather, Charles Schweitzer, for mistreating his mother. Sartre's autobiography is a biting, aggressive attack on his parents and grandparents. Not only was he aggressive to his father and grandfather, but he also hated his childhood. He said, "I hated my childhood and everything that remained from it." Owing to the hatred he felt for his roots, Sartre endeavored to formulate a philosophical system that created a gap between himself and his roots. I suggest that no one can ever succeed in putting a void between the human family and the Great Father without destroying the structure. Existence without the Great Father is devoid of rules and regulations that govern the human family. Without the Great Father, we are without ethics and morals. Interestingly, Sartre offered only two laws, which are contradictory in terms—authenticity and inauthenticity. Inauthenticity is a bad faith. It is self-deception—deceiving yourself that you are not free to make choices. Authenticity is an acknowledgement that I alone freely choose what I do and I alone am responsible for the consequences of my choices. This philosophy tends to lead to antinomianism. Antinomianism leads to anarchy. Anarchy ushers in human suffering.

Nevertheless, I agree with Sartre that pain can be a means to wisdom and freedom. As we have seen, the ordeals that an individual experienced during circumcision gave him a greater freedom—freedom of being an adult and a part of his age group and of learning all the secrets of the tribe. For a kikuyu, passing through Kikuyu wisdom and instruction, which were attained during the initiation, was not a matter of choice. One was condemned to initiation to tribal wisdom. The wisdom was acquired through suffering in total silence on circumcision day and utter submission to the sponsors during the ordeals of seclusion period.

The suffering was intended to produce an individual who could think philosophically, who was guided by reason rather than feelings, who does not act impulsively on the first feeling he experiences in response to a situation, but who examines that situation from different perspectives. This person was usually guided not so much by passions of the moment, although he may take them into account, but by realities of the situation, the goal he is pursuing, and the principles and values that he found trustworthy. He does not chronically deny his emotions, but does not precipitously give in to them. The wise person does not totally desert the cave, but unlike other chained prisoners, he broke the chain and had courage to moving outside of the cave so as to face the pleasure of sunshine and beauty of the world as well as the pains of storms, hurricanes, and earthquakes of life. He was far from being narcissistic. He did not have extreme self-love and excessive preoccupation with himself and his own concerns. He made fewer demands on others to satisfy his own pride and wishes. He avoided causing needless suffering to others and to himself also.

Pain, if taken as an initiation, bears positive fruits. It can be redemptive to the sufferers and others. The cross, which is the most significant symbol of the Christian, narrates the story of God who suffered in order to redeem the whole world. The cross is a symbol of God's love—"God shows his love to us for while we were yet sinners Christ died for us."

Thus, in counseling and therapy, we need to be aware of the positive as well as negative aspects of pain. As Josef Gold Brunner observes, "While a pastor should know joy, he must know pain as well, for pain is the element of our salvation-situation. More exactly it is the element most impressive and palpable to man and consequently seems to be predominant in pastoral care."

More often than not, people go to pastors and therapists because of pain. The great temptation of the healing team is to shorten the liminality of life in order to reduce the pain. We should, however, ask the following questions: How can I facilitate learning and growth? How can I enable the sufferer to find himself in the wilderness? How can I illuminate the hurting person so that he may find God in the marginal entity? How can the painful situation lead to self-examination and self-determination? How can the present pain facilitate moral and ethical growth? How can the anguish led the sufferer to maturity and wisdom?

E. PAIN AND TREATMENT

However, the pastors and counselors who work with those who undergo through painful rites of passage may go through unnecessary pain. They may believe that it is only the bitter medicine that heals. They may believe that: "Nothing good that comes from a good place." In medical treatment, they may prefer an injection to a capsule. In extreme cases they may reduce the present life to pain and suffering in the hope of getting the brightest future. They may also accept to suffer unnecessary pain. Mugo Gatheru, a Kikuyu student at an American College experienced unnecessary pain when he dated an American girl who had an artificial plate of front teeth. During kissing, Gatheru put his tongue in the girl's mouth. Since her gum did not have sensation, her teeth fell on his tongue. In Gatheru`s words: "I felt pain since she was actually biting me and it was exceedingly painful… but outwardly I made it appear as if I was enjoying it. In the end, the kissing was over! I excused myself to go to the lavatory to spit some blood from my tongue."

The reader cannot fail to see a parallel between Mugo's attitude to the kissing session and his attitude to the knife, which cut him during the circumcision. Although the kissing was exceedingly painful, he did not show any feeling of pain. He made it appear as though he was enjoying it. He behaved the same way during the pain of the knife: "It was very, very painful," he says, "but I did not show any feeling of fear or even act as if I were being cut." Mugo being unconsciously influenced by the irua experience, accepted unnecessary pain. What Gatheru did is typical of many kikuyu. For this reason, when giving pastoral care and counseling to those who are suffering, the priest should try to find out whether or not the suffering is worthy.

It also has to be pointed out that a kikuyu regards tears as a sign of fear, rejection of pain, and a denial of circumcision. For this reason, they do not understand the positivity of tears in releasing emotional tension. Unfortunately, some bereaved Kikuyu suffer from what psychiatrists' term "hypochondria," an abnormal condition characterized by a depressed emotional state. As we have noted, in old days, the bereaved persons released their emotions through sexual intercourse. The widows employed "sword sellers" who slept with them and had sexual intercourse twice a night. Subsequently, these sword sellers became their life-long sexual partners. Interestingly, this custom is still in the deep structure of the Kikuyu mind. A few weeks ago, some Kikuyu friends and I were discussing modern Kikuyu funerals. One of my friends expressed his surprising experience during the wake. "I visited the bereaved at night," he said. "I found many people in the house. Other people were in the yard. After staying in the house for a while I went out to see what was happening. I was astonished to see men and women lying on the grass making love." Dominated by that part of them, which is ancestral, which goes back thousands of years (C.G. Jung terms this realm of personality "Objective Psyche"), the Kikuyu may use sexuality to release their emotion during bereavement. However, they find themselves in tension between their past, which is still in them, and the Christian ethic that condemns any sexual affair outside marriage. The church should give alternative means of releasing the emotion; we need to tell them that tears are one of the most valuable things that God has given us. It purges our psyche and releases our sorrow.

As we have noted, during the circumcision, one is not expected to show any feeling of fear. Gatheru told us how he bravely sat down and folded his fists as a boxer. He also told us about his awareness of the expectation of the crowd, "The crowd was very silent," he says, "waiting perhaps to detect whether I would show a sense of feeling of fear." As Gatheru indicated, a Kikuyu fears his fear. He may fear that his fear will be detected. A circumcised Kikuyu equates the showing of fear with de-circumcision. The priest and counselors need to help the Kikuyu to get in touch with their fear. Fear is a part of human nature. Each person has a particular person, or place or object that can evoke his fear. It is spiritually and psychologically healthy to know the objects that evoke one's fear and to acknowledge them. My own philosophy, which is too costly to be sold to other people, is this: I look at my fear, talk to it, and love it. I pay attention to the places, persons, and things that trigger my fear and admire them. This philosophy has helped me to turn my fear into a friend. I love my fear because it has saved me from being a giant or a super man who cannot empathize with other people.

In conclusion, we have seen that pain may have physical, spiritual, and psychological causes. It may bear negative results; namely mistrust, doubt, shame, guilt, ego-diffusion, inferiority feeling, self-absorption, stagnation, despair, withdrawal, insanity, and death. It can also have a positive effect such as trust, autonomy, industry, identity, intimacy, generativity, integrity, joy, and exaltation. It was the Kikuyu's positive attitude toward pain that encouraged them to suffer and die for their land, freedom and their faith in Jesus Christ in the 1950s. Joy and pain are interwoven in our earthly pilgrimage. Pain is real! The events of pain have a course, like the biological aging process, that continuously influences man…and its movement can be rendered fruitful through a conscious acceptance and formation.

As we have seen, betrayal causes intensive pain and so we will turn to this subject.

CHAPTER 20

BETRAYAL

Even my close friend, whom I trusted,
He who I shared my bread,
Has lifted up his heel against me.
—Psalm 41:9

Did you know wherever Satan want to hurt you most he uses a friend whom you trust or a member of your family? Did know Judas who had to betray Jesus, was entrust the most important office-finance.

Which we regard as lifeblood? Did you know the name Judas and Jude? (the brother of Jesus who wrote Jude) are the same? Thus, Jesus grew with that name which has eventually to betray him. Did you know that David, the writer of the above message was hunted by his father in law?

So, my friend, if you had or are being betrayed by a member of your family or a close friend, you need to know that you are not alone. The same happened to David. Not only that David was betrayed by his father in law, but also by his most handsome son,

Absalom. Moreover, he gathered together a group which had to overturn the government. The challenger was so great that David had to cry out to God:

> Save me oh God,
> For the water had come up to my neck,
> In sink into the mirely depth,
> Where there is no foot hold
> I have come into the deep waters
> The floods engulf me.
> … I am forced to restore what I did not steal Psalm 69:1–2, 4

As you read this this message, there is a faithful servant of God who is going through fire. You may be being betrayed by a close friend of a member of your family. This hurts greatly; but it should not be an excuse for not trusting the Lord. Stay plugged in Him. Don't lose your integrity. Pray with the Psalmist: "In my integrity you uphold me and set me in your presence." He also assured that if you stay plugged in the Universal Spiritual energy, you are unconquerable. So, you need to sooth your soul with God's word: "The Lord is my light and my salvation whom shall fear? The Lord is the stronghold of my life of whom shall I be afraid." Psalm 27: More importantly, let the Holy Spirit fill every fiber of your being and he will fill you with his power, joy and peace. What does our precious Lord advise us to to when you are insulted and falsely accused: "Blessed are you when people insult you, persecute you and falsely say all kinds of veil against you because of me. Rejoice and be glad because the great is your reward in heaven, for in the same way they persecuted the prophet who were before you." Matthew 5:11–12.

This joy will make you and your family be firmly rooted to the Tree of God, the Great Mother and the Great Father.

CHAPTER 21

THE TREE OF GOD

A. DEFINITION OF THE TERM

As we have noted, the name kikuyu derives from Mukuyu tree. This is due to the fact that, according to our myth, Kikuyu, the father of the tribe, emerged from the roots of the fig tree. Thus, the genesis of the Kikuyu people is associated with the tree. This tree will be termed the Tree of God.

As we have mentioned, the liminal entity included the rite under the tree whereby the senior adviser took beer and poured it around the tree, took some honey and smeared it onto it, and then prayed to Murungu, the ancestral God who transcends all that is. He then took the milk juice from the tree and marked the male initiates on their cheeks, around the eyes, the center of their foreheads, hands, and legs. Then the wife of the senior adviser put the milk juice on both of the girls' temples, on their necks, on their nipples, and their hands. Symbolically, this rite connected the initiates with the Tree of God out of which Kikuyu, the father of the tribe came.

Under the Tree of God, they were attached to the mystical sacred time when the Supreme Being was present on earth and mystically revealed himself, in human form, to the father of the tribe. They were also conjoined with Ngai, the Supreme Being and the Great Provider, with other mystical beings, the ancestors and the cosmos.

Thus, the term Tree of God will be used to denote that which is in our inner world, which connects us with our primordial time, the Supreme Being, the mystical beings, the ancestors and the mysteries around us. We will also use it for the external phenomenon, objects, insects, and animals that make us aware of this inner reality.

The Tree of God is located in man's "Garden of Eden." It comprises "the tree of the knowledge of good and evil" and "the tree of life," which sustains the human soul. It is the object and subject of people's myths, legends, sagas, proverbs, and idioms. It is the meeting point of Anthropos (humanity) and the shekinah (the dwelling of God with his own). Under the Tree of God, we are made aware of the totality of our humanity and the presence of the God, who is the possessor of brightness and who-shines-in Holiness. It also makes us aware of the totality of our environment and our awareness of being and the complexity and the ambiguity of life. Like the ark of the covenant, the Tree of God has both healing and destructive powers (here).

B. THE COMMUNAL TREE

We have noted that there is an object that makes an individual aware of the Tree of God. This we shall term an individual tree. In addition, there is an object that makes a particular community aware of the Tree of God. This we shall term the communal tree. For the Kikuyu, the communal tree was the sacred tree which was set apart for Ngai known as muti wa Ngai (the Tree of God). Under this tree, God was worshipped. The tree itself was never worshipped, but it was regarded as sacred and one would not have dared to cut its branches or twigs—or approach it alone at night.

The Fruitful Family

The Kikuyu people project their inner Tree of God to a chameleon, which they revere and fear more than a totem. Let me illustrate. On one occasion, I put a chameleon in a box, covered it with a lid, and took the reptile to a class that consisted of Kikuyu students and students from other ethnic groups. I told the students that I had something in the box that I would take around and that I would uncover the lid as I approached every student. I instructed the students should touch what was in the box without informing other students what they had seen and touched. Interestingly, students from other ethnic groups touched the creature without showing any change of facial expression. But whenever a Kikuyu student saw the animal, he/she was moved to a great sensation of awe. They expressed a sensation similar to that of Adam and Eve when they heard the sound of the Lord God walking in the garden in the cool of the day after they had eaten the forbidden fruit. After the exhibition, I asked the Kikuyu students to talk about the chameleon. One of the students narrated, "Once upon a time, when God created human beings, he told the chameleon, 'Go and tell people, you shall never die!' As God was talking to the chameleon, the lizard overheard and outran the slow walking reptile and reach the people first and gave them the message of death. The lizard told the people, 'God has said, thou shall surely die and perish.' This is why we die," concluded the student.

After the class, I spent hours with the chameleon in my backyard. I studied its behavior and discovered that it is both swift and slow. Even though it approached the environment stealthily, whenever it saw a prey, its long tongue moved as fast as a bullet. It never missed an insect. It changes its colors not only to conceal itself from the enemy, but also to remain incognito in the presence of the prey. I discovered that the chameleon is one of the most intuitive animals that God has created.

As with the chameleon, the Kikuyu people are extremely intuitive and adaptable. In their search for economic freedom, they possess almost selfless dedication. They have propensity for compromise whenever they perceive that they will benefit from a situation.

Thus, the chameleon is a creature that makes this community conscious of their ontology, their genesis, the origin of life and death, the anthropomorphic God who appeared to their forefathers and mothers, and the ambiguity of life. Put differently, the chameleon mirrors their psychic archetype that I term as the Tree of God.

For many people of the world, a priest or a Shaman is an outward object on which they project their inner Tree of God. The priest, as a mana person, represents powers, which can uproot, pull down, destroy, and overthrow. These powers are also capable of building, planting, nurturing, and sustaining. The mana person symbolizes healing and destructive powers. As a therapeutic symbol, the priest is the means of grace. As a negative symbol, the priest represents here, which can throw people to the darkness of God in order to usher them into the glorious light of the Deity-who-shines-in-holiness. He mirrors people's morals and makes them conscious of their moral strength as well as their short-comings. The priest may provoke a dreadful feeling or fear of the Holy, just as a chameleon makes the Kikuyu aware of the ancestral God. When I was a teenager, we had a parish priest known as Peter Owit, whom we nicknamed "Peter the Rock." Physically, Peter the Rock was a huge man. In addition, the Rock had enormous spiritual energy. His physical and spiritual energy compelled him to move like a lion. One day Peter the Rock, in his priestly collar, paid a surprise visit to the biggest beer hall in town. He dashed in and found hundreds of people drinking beer. Seeing a priest, some people were confounded with awe, threw their mugs of beer on the floor, and ran away. The presence of Peter the Rock evoked the same feeling as the chameleon evoked to the Kikuyu students.

The late professor Urban T. Holmes, III, an American priest who was my teacher and supervisor of my doctoral dissertation, reported an incident, which was similar to that of Peter the Rock. Dr. Holmes, when he was a chaplain in the university, visited students in their dormitory and found them drinking beer. When a student saw the priest, he gasped, "Oh my God!" whirled around, and leapt out of the window.

The Fruitful Family

The two illustrations indicate how the priests from two different cultures and hemispheres elicited the similar feeling. They evoked a feeling of awe, just as the chameleon does to the Kikuyu people. It suffices, therefore, to conclude that priests, rabbis, shaman, and other religious specialists are external objects on which the communities mirror their inner.

Other external communal Trees of God include shrines such as church buildings, temples, mosques, and tribal sacred objects, such as sacred mountains, trees, stones, animals, and rivers.

There are also cosmic central Trees of God, which are centripetal for peoples of many cultures, languages, tribes, nationalities, and continents. These cosmic communal trees of God are golden threads, which bind all people together. They give our inner tree of God, which is at the center of our garden of Eden, a feeling of wholeness. For the Roman Catholic, Rome and the Pope are the cosmic central Trees of God. The Anglican Communion has Canterbury and the Archbishop of Canterbury, Jerusalem is the cosmic central Tree of God for all Christians. The Muslims have Mecca as their central tree of God.

The above holy places and persons are centripetal, which magnetizes the human families to the cosmic center. They redeem them from centrifugal forces, which pull them away from the axis. They are indeed analogous to the psychic archetype of the Tree of God, which is located in the center of humankind's garden of Eden.

C. THE INDIVIDUAL TREES

THE EXTERNAL INDIVIDUAL TREES MAY be as many as there are individuals. My own individual tree is a mole. For me, this creature is more than an animal. Its very presence touches my collective unconscious. Our daughter's individual tree is a dog. My wife and I became aware of this when she was three and a half and started developing an awareness of the presence of dogs. She was particularly scared by black furry dogs. When this happened, we remembered how she first found a black dog in my study room when she was two and a half years old. On that occasion she was not scared, but remembered the dog for many years.

At the age of four, she developed a great fear of dogs. Unfortunately, we were living at Sewanee, Tennessee where there were almost as many dogs as there were people. One could not walk for five minutes without meeting a dog. This meant that Rehema had to scream several times a day. This scared us since we were the only African family in that area and Rehema was the only black child in kindergarten. Since her school was also peopled with dogs, she screamed constantly and scared other children and the teachers. While her fear for the dog was becoming greater, my wife and I tried hard to reconcile her with the dogs. I took her to the dog, which she first met in my study room. I had given her a warning in good time so she did not cry when we found the dog. In its presence, I started telling a story.

"Once upon a time there was an African girl living at Sewanee. On one occasion she entered her daddy's study room and saw a dog."

"That girl is me," she interrupted.

"And this is the dog. It is not as black as you. It is as black as me." From this dialogue I learned that there was a real connection between her blackness and the dog, her African root and this totem. As a result of this awareness, Mary and I decided to have a black girl as Rehema's baby sitter. We got Linda, a disabled girl who was as black as Rehema. So, we had to take Rehema to Linda's home. To our surprise, when she saw the black faces of Linda's family, she screamed in the same way as she did in the presence of the dogs. However, we forced her to be looked after by Linda, and after six weeks she stopped crying. Linda and her family became her friends. Interestingly, this lessened her fear of dogs. In further attempts to reconcile Rehema with her individual tree, Mary took her picture when she was in the nude. But when she saw her photograph for the first time, she demonstrated the same feeling as she had for the dogs. After this, we got a black furry dog for her. For seven weeks, she either worshipped the dog or screamed at it. During the seventh week she said she did not want the dog because it was scaring her. Instead of accepting her request, Mary locked her and the dog in her bedroom. Rehema cried and cried until she was tired and then slept. She spent that night with her puppy. This incident not only ended her screaming at dogs, she also developed a positive attitude toward her African roots. She started saying to her American friends: "I am an African girl." And whenever we met a dog, she said, "I don't fear you anymore. You are my friend." However, for her, dogs are more than animals.

At the age of six and a half years, she told us about her creation myth. She narrated: "In the beginning, God created dogs, then the light, and then the trees. And finally, he created 214 The Tree of God people." The dogs seem to connect her with the mystical and primordial time.

While the above illustrations clarify my point about external communal and individual trees, they have almost over simplified the meaning of the tree. The external trees are symbols. Symbols are not signs. Symbols emerge from and reach the unconscious. They reveal the unknown and unknowable. While signs speak to the intellect, symbols capture the whole person.

As we have seen, Kikuyu, the father, and the hero of the tribe, emerged from the tree. He was born out of the tree. Thus, the tree is also a symbol of the Great Mother.

C.G. Jung rightly contends that the tree of life is a common mother-symbol and that it may have been, in first instance, a fruit-bearing genealogical tree, hence a kind of tribal mother. He observed that numerous myths say that human beings came from trees and many of them tell how the hero was enclosed in the maternal tree. This is true to the Kikuyu myth, which relates the origin of the first man with the tree. The tree, the tribal mother, existed before the father of the tribe. Thus, the tree is also one of the symbols of the Great Mother to whom we now turn.

CHAPTER 22

THE GREAT MOTHER

The term great mother refers to the feminine quality which is predominant in women, but which is also found in a fully functioning male person. The archetypical motif of great mother is found in mythology and human history. She has both positive and negative aspects.

A. THE MYTH AND REALITY OF THE GREAT MOTHER

THE KIKUYU MYTH INCLUDES TWO great women. The first one is Mumbi, the mother of the tribe and wife of Kikuyu, who had nine daughters and no sons. The name Mumbi means the creator and the molder.

The other woman hero is Wangu wa Makeri, who, unlike Mumbi, is both a historical and a mythical figure. Mythically, Wangu was a very successful warrior and a judge. But when she was at the peak of her reign, she became arrogant and danced naked. This act provoked men's anger and consequently she was dethroned. This ended the woman's reign in Kikuyu land.

The Fruitful Family

However, I have interviewed several people in order to get historical facts about Wangu. According to James Makeri, the grandson of Wangu, the husband of Wangu, Makeri, was a very wealthy man. He had a big land, a large number of livestock, and men servants. He was also a man of great integrity. For these reasons he was respected by the Chief Justice Karuri wa Gakure. The former provided the latter with lodging on his way to Muranag's. Consequently, they became great friends and, thus, Karuri requested Makeri whether he would like to be made a judge. Makeri refused and said that he would rather take care for his wealth, but recommended Wangu to Karuri. He informed Karuri that Wangu was a woman of great integrity and had leadership quality. Thus, Wangu was made the leader. Eventually Wangu gained respect and became famous for her leadership. She had a strong army, which fought and won many battles. However, she only fought those who refused to comply with Karuri. The songs were composed about her victory. These songs were also urging those people who had not submitted to her to surrender to her and to the senior chief.

Muchiri Makeri, the stepson of Wangu argued thatWhat made Wangu famous was not the battles which she fought and won, but her work of reconciliation. She reconciled Karuri with many Kikuyu families. On the one hand she persuaded people to support the chief justice and on the other, she persuaded Karuri not to fight those who were not rebels and those who had surrendered. In most cases, it was Wangu who ended the war by her diplomatic way of persuasion and reconciliation.

In addition, Wangu's home was a house of refuge. If someone committed a crime such as murder and was chased by people in order to be arrested and be killed, if he could run and reach Wangu's home before he was caught, that man was safe. Thus, Wangu saved many people who could have been killed. Another activity that made Wangu famous was the saving of innocent children who were being thrown to the hyena. According to the Kikuyu custom, if a woman gave birth to twins, their mouths were filled with grass and they were thrown to the bush to be devoured by the hyena. If a mother with a baby who was less than one year old died, the baby and the body of the deceased were taken to the bush to be consumed by the hyena. So Wangu wa Makeri ventured a new mission of saving these children. She instructed her soldiers how to save these children. The men had to wrestle with the hyena in order to save a baby. All the babies who were rescued were brought to Wangu's home where they were cared for by her. Muchiri said, "My main duty when I was a boy was to feed those babies with milk." Here we can see that Wangu was a forerunner of various organizations and institutions in Kenya, which are caring for destitute children.

Furthermore, Wangu was one of the first African leaders to realize that the first missionaries had something that was beneficial to the country. She studied McGregor of Weithaga Mission, her neighbor and found that he had something useful to offer– education. So, she took some of the orphans to him. She urged her people, particularly those who were poor, to take their children to the missionary school. She also reconciled the missionaries with the chief justice. When she was reaching death, Wangu became a Christian and was baptized.

According to those who witnessed the dance, Wangu never danced naked. She had four pieces: the inner soft leather that covered her private part, an apron that covered her upper part, the skirt (Muthuru), and a long garment that covered her from neck to ankle known as riba, which is a long ceremonial dress like a long overcoat. It was this ceremonial dress, which Wangu removed in order that she could dance freely. Normally, one could not dance with a ceremonial dress.

Thus, Wangu was famous, not because of dancing naked, but owing to her hospitality, love, ministry of reconciliation, and transforming of Kikuyu tradition. She had the qualities of the ideal Great Mother.

The Fruitful Family

B. THE POSITIVITY OF THE GREAT MOTHER:

THE GREAT MOTHER AS AN archetype creates and repairs human relationships. She helps us to reach out, to join, to get in touch with, and be involved in concrete feelings, things, and people. She does not allow us to hang in the air, but pushes us right into the middle of events and things. Instead of being detached she involves us and urges us to be a part of happenings. She attracts us to the mode of being and relatedness.

In addition, the Great Mother connects us with our tradition. It is this essence that draws us to our mother-land so that we may be connected with our roots. It magnetizes us by in-going rather than out-going and then leads us to the dark womb in order that we may be reborn. By restating us, the Great Mother generates new intuitions, fantasies, images, and drives. When this precious work is taking place, the images of water, home, cooking pot, cave, ark, coffin, and mountain appear in our dreams and fantasies.

And as we have seen in the myth of the Kikuyu female chief, the archetype of the Great Mother allows us to be mararanja. The story that narrates that Wangu danced naked expresses this quality, which is inherent in human personality. This archetype allows us to be irrational, ecstatic, and non-moralistic. Its dynamism pushes us outside of the self and sets us free from the tribal taboos. It was this dynamism that drove Wangu to a mission of saving the babies, which were thrown to the hyenas. Saving these innocent twins was against the social norm of the time. The same dynamism empowered great men like William Wilberforce and Abraham Lincoln in their war against slavery.

This quality of the Great Mother allows us to be emotionally involved, to take risks, and, thereby, enlarge our ego boundaries. It inspires us and fills us with vitality. It throws us to the forces, which are above and beyond our limitations.

The Great Mother is the source of life and nourishment. In her and through her, an individual is soothed, comforted, and cherished. Nyumba (the mother's house) in which she dwells is the theatre of riddles, stories, and jokes. In this dwelling, an individual is free to be what Urban T. Holmes termed as a receptive mode of human consciousness. This mode of consciousness as opposed to action mode, processes experience in spatial images, in concrete rather than abstract ways, in holistic or relational over analytical or differentiated modes, in nonlinear terms rather than linear, analogically and not digitally, and through intuitive thinking as opposed to rational thought.

C. NEGATIVITY OF THE GREAT MOTHER

WHEN THE GREAT MOTHER GETS sick, she expresses qualities that are opposed to those of a healthy one. Instead of being a refuge for her children, she devours them when they come to her for rescue. She scatters her children. She becomes impatient and does not allow her children to be in dark womb for nine months. She forces them out before a successful rebirth. And thus, they fail to move from one developmental stage to another. Said differently, the sick Great Mother has no patience for being with her children for forty years in the wilderness. She kills them before they have reached the Promised Land.

In addition, the sick mother may feel insecure and thus overprotect her children and deprive them mararanja expression, which facilitates the expansion of ego boundaries and self-transcendence. She makes their lives static, rigid, and boring.

In addition to the house of the sick Great Mother, is the theatre of gossip and agitation. It is this sickness that is expressed by a Kikuyu proverb, "Women have no upright words, but only crooked ones". By her crooked words, the sick mother leads her children from light to darkness, from patient and love to uncontrollable anger, from repairing of relationship to destruction of human relationship, from sobriety to drunkenness, from self-identity to ego diffusion, and from sanity to insanity.

The healthy Great Mother, as we have seen, has a quality of reconciliation, relatedness, rebirth, traditionality, dynamism, and vitality. She repairs broken relationship. She is more interested in friendship. She values relationship more than riches. She makes every effort to reconcile her children with the Great Father.

CHAPTER 23

THE GREAT FATHER

The term Great Father will refer to the male aspect of human nature, which is predominately in men, but also found in fully functioning woman. The archetypal motif of the Great Father is evident in myths, idioms, and proverbs. He has both negative and positive aspects.

Structure and emotionlessness, which are the attributes of the Great Father, were demonstrated and ritualized on the actual day of circumcision. As we have seen, even the girls were not supposed to show any fear or make any audible sign of emotion or even blink. During the summit of pain, she demonstrated fearlessness. She was expected to be highly structured. The male initiated was expected to show the same mannerism. All the initiates were challenged by the Great Father to be highly structured and to confront fear and pain with courage.

Since initiation dominated an individual from birth to death, this quality of the Great Father rained from childhood to death. I have always been astonished at this quality in one of my sisters. Mary cared for me when I was a baby and a little boy. To my surprise, I have never seen her crying. Occasionally, when she was a little girl, my father would pinch her ear lobe and cause bleeding, but Mary never cried or even showed any emotion. She manifested the same bravely in defending me against any prey. One day, when we were herding, a boy who was bigger than Mary wanted to attack us, but Mary aimed at his forehead with a club, hit the boy, and knocked him down. I was amused the following day when the father of the boy came to report to my mother (this time my father had gone to glory) that Mary injured his son.

The other day, at age of sixty-eight, I reminded Mary of this incident. She bragged, "Even today, I am not yet old, and I do not allow anybody to step on my toes." This quality of life is typical to boys and girls who are unconsciously dominated by the actual day of circumcision. Since the archetype of the Great Father is within the collective unconscious, its quality is not limited to those who are initiated. It is inherent in uninitiated women as well. It is, indeed, found in all human families.

A. HIS DWELLING PLACES

THE GREAT FATHER DWELLS IN thingira (a traditional father's house). In father's house, one is challenged to be assertive and intentional. Here, mararanja dances are halted. The favorite proverb of the Great Father is, "Thiga has been circumcised, no more mararanja." Meaning, since he is already circumcised, there is no more irrationality. This calls for economy of time and words. It also challenges and individual to be economically minded and precise.

While the Great Mother prefers stories, analogies, and metaphors, the Great Father favors a clear and logical language. The Great Mother entices us to be subjective. The Great Father urges us to be objective.

He enjoys sitting in parliament and in congress where he makes laws by which he governs and guides his children, in law courts where he judges and imprisons those who break the law, and in prison where he rehabilitates those whom he has imprisoned.

The Fruitful Family

Since the qualities of the great father are in both male and female, we do not, therefore, imply that the above institutions are or should be dominated by males. However, it is my argument that it is the qualities of the Great Father which are dominant in these institutions. To illustrates: During the staff institute of Association Institution of Theological Institutions of East Africa which I have already mentioned, I was in a team, which had to visit Arusha International Conference Center. After reaching this gigantic building, we were led to an office where we had to get someone who could take us around. Unfortunately, there was no one in the office. Consequently, we waited for several minutes. In the meantime, we were attracted by a chart on the wall, which included the pictures of all the government ministers. For those of us who were not Tanzanian, it took us as a surprise to note that the official title of the ministers is Ndugu (Brother). Interestingly, there were pictures of two women ministers whose titles were Ndugu. These were Ndugu Jullie C. Manning, Wasiri wa Sheria (Brother Jullie C. Mnanning, the Minister of Law, and Ndugu Tabitha Siwale, Waziri wa Elimu ya Taifa (Brother Tabith Siwale, Minister for National Education. The use of the title Ndugu for a woman minister appeared to us as a contradiction in terms. However, our Tanzania friends informed us that the word Ndugu in this context meant a comrade. This was not convincing since the word Dada (Sister) could also convey the same meaning. Symbolically, I believe, the title Ndugu refers to the substance of the Great Father who makes laws and implement them in the government administration.

B. THE SUBSTANCE OF THE GREAT FATHER

WISDOM IS ANOTHER PROPERTY OF the Great Father. Interestingly, the Kikuyu ascribe all wise expressions, idioms, and proverbs to the father of the tribe. For this reason, whenever someone is using a proverb, he must credit the father of the tribe; it goes this way, "Kikuyu said, The day is for working, the night is for resting." It is as though the first father coined all the proverbs that guides the tribe in their daily living. The Great Father possesses the logos, which is the subtle fire emanating the whole universe. This logos is characterized by fire or light. This light illumines and guides the human family. Initiative, assertiveness, creativity, and objectivity are other traits of the Great Father. He challenges us to venture into new projects, to declare our standpoint, and to be ourselves. He admonishes us not to waste time with petty things. He challenges us to be and to allow others to be.... He challenges us to be ourselves with a proverb: "One does not structure his family as that of his age mate." This meant that even though the age set underwent the same school, every person was an individual. For that reason, the Kikuyu discouraged over-identification. A person who aped another person was rebuked. If for instance, Mwangi noticed that Njoroge was over-identifying himself with Kamau, Mwangi would shout, "Kamau identification!" (Kamau Kanyi), meaning, you are not yourself but a false Kamau. Thus, the Great Father urges us to be ourselves.

In his negative expression, the Great Father may ignore the collective responsibility and concentrate on his own personal interest. For instance, the Great Father in the parliament may use his influential position as a means of appropriating wealth and oppressing the community that has voted for him. He may become corrupt and ignore the law. He may defend the "haves" and deny justice to the "have-nots."

The Great Father may become power-thirsty and unreachable to his children. In this negativity, he becomes as a lion or an elephant that crushes to death those who may be the future leaders. He may become autocratic and have no interest in consensus of opinion. This destructive behavior creates a personality that is more interested in power than progress.

The sick Great Father may be imbued with aggression and wreck his family. In this case, he became moody and always attacking children, depriving them of freedom of expression and being, which are necessary for personality development. He may also order his children to attack other people and spend government revenue with unnecessary wars. In so doing he provokes other nations to war. This may result to global recession. In this case, the Great Father ignores other aspect to life so as to equip his hunting dogs.

When he gets sick, the Great Father may ignore his own responsibilities and take the responsibility of others. To use a Kikuyu proverbs, "He roofs other people's huts while his own hut is leaking," "He disregards his own log while he tries to take the speck from his neighbor's eye," "He attributes all the goodness and strength in the community to himself while projecting his garbage to others," "Instead of repenting his own sin he tries to convince the whole world that all evil resides in those around him."

Another negative aspect of the Great Father is *absent farness.* By absent farness I refer to a permanent removal of the father's house from the homestead, and building it in a far country. In this case, the father is permanently away from the family. He leaves his family in the countryside and goes to the town to earn a living. This mode of life is becoming the order of the day in Kenya. The degree of absent farness varies. Some husbands who live away from their families may visit their home once a month or once a year to take some money, and of course to manufacture more children to whom they will never give day-to-day guidance and emotional support. Others stay in their working place with concubines or prostitutes and, therefore, squander all their money. They may stay for years without visiting their families. The extreme category is that of the husbands who have totally deserted their families with no hope of being reunited again. The last category is that of the families who do not know what it is to have a father. The mother has never been married, yet she has a family of which she is the head and a potential provider. Needless to say, the case of absentee fathers is crucial in East Africa. It has been estimated that 60 percent of the husbands do not stay with their families. This is a new phenomenon, since traditionally the father's dwelling was located within the homestead. Here he guided, protected, and sustained the family. His sons and daughters had someone to imitate. They had a father who could enforce discipline. At present the majority of the mothers are left alone with their children. In most cases, they are both the bread winners and the heads of families. In all cases of absentee fathers, the mother is in charge of the day to day running of the family. She is the head of the family. This issue of the absenteeism of fathers is indeed ushering in a new era in African society. We are possibly in a transitional period, moving from a patriarchal society to a matriarchal society. This society will have a real problem with the authority figures. It will have no respect for the rule of the law, which is the product of the Great Father. Possibly, this society will find it easier to unite behind a system rather than a person.

The sick Great Father may be unforgiving and legalistic, expecting his children not only to obey every code of law but also may expect them to live in accordance with his whims. He may also be too involved and, therefore, pay little attention to trivial matters. He may be hunting for gossip and rumor and use them as criteria for judging and punishing his children. This type of involvement is what we term *destructive nearness*. When the Great Father has this type of nearness, he deprives his children of freedom of expression and of being, which is vital for their ego development. He robs them of wisdom, which is acquired through trial and error.

In conclusion, the positive qualities of the Great Father include structure, assertiveness, intentionality, judgment, rehabilitation, wisdom, initiative, and creativity. His negative characteristics are comprised of aggressiveness, absent farness, destructive nearness, irresponsibility, legalism and, authoritarianism.

We avoid the negative qualities by being in Christ who claim: "I am the vine; you are the branches. He who abide in me and I in him, he it is that bear much fruits, for apart from me you can do nothing. John 15: St. Paul has the best definition of the fruit that Christ is talking about. He wrote: "But the fruits of the spirit is love, joy peace, patience, kindness, goodness, faithfulness, gentleness and self-control. Galatians 5:22 The saint has this fruit and it is this quality of life which attracted people to Christ.

CHAPTER 24

WE ARE THE FRUITS OF THE SAINTS

November includes the commemoration of all Saints and all faithful souls. The Saints included the well-known Christian who paid the ultimate price for their faithfulness and willing to die for their faith and witness. The all faithful souls include un canonized witness and prophets. The Saints includes Paul who was chained and died like criminal. In both category we have great men like William Tyndale, who were burned at stake for translating the Bible in English, Hugh Latina and Nicholas Radley for starting renewal in England in 1555. Their mission statement was: "We shall light that fire in England as shall never be extinguished." They were accused of "protestantizing" and were burned at stake by the regime of Bloody Queen Mary. Even though they were brutally killed, the fire which they had lit was not extinguished. It eventually spread to East African and started East Africa revival movement which lit fire in me. And all the people that God has won to himself through me Hugh and Nicholas will receive a reward. We should also commemorate Abraham Lincoln who died for defending the union between Northern and Southern state and abolition of slavery. So, it was through the dedication of Abraham Lincoln that I am a missionary in North America.

Similarly, we should remember Stephen Biko, leader of black consciousness in South Africa. By strengthening the ego of his community, he was lock in cell without toilet, sleeping on his urine, and when he became sick, he was transported to the hospital on a truck naked and of course he died nicked. Stephen message was "The sense of defeat is what we are against." His message did not die with him. He became one of the fathers on Black Theology. This theology might have inspired Baraka Obama whose mission statement was: "Yes we can."

All Saint and All Souls days challenges us to have a mission statement. The mission statement of ANCCI is: "empowered by the Holy Spirit, we preach the gospel to all nations." As a theologian and cultural anthropologist, I have been awed by unique cultural ethos of the nations that I minister. I was surprised when I landed at Manila airport, in Philippines to met someone who introduce a motion for debate. We were total strangers. The motion was Vatican 1 verses Vatican 2. I argued for the Vatican 2 while he defended Vatican 1. We argued for 30 minutes. After which I asked him whether he was a theologian. He informed me that He was agriculture Officer. I was pleased by the way we debated without being angry. Another debate was started by a bishop who hosted us after I had consecrated his son, and Ordain several women who included his daughter in law. What amazed me was that the women, who were serving us were the one I have just ordained. But the debate gave me a golden opportunity of walking the audience throw the Bible on women ministry and leadership Starting with Debora, who was a judge and the prophet to Mary Magdalene who was the first Apostle. After the debate, one lady said: "for your information the wife of the man who is debating with you was a pastor."

The Saints undergo through exaltation and humiliation. In August on 2001 I participated in mission to Panama which was organed by the Episcopal church for minority exposure to mission.

The Fruitful Family

We were a team of 8. All the missioners who included African American and native Americans were fair color. I was the only one who was black with three doctorates. To my greatest surprise, I was held with great honor by the Panamas. On one occasion the team attended entertainment. I was surprised by someone who came to me opening his mouth and pointing to his tooth saying: "You are a doctor. Please help me. I have a toothache." I later learned that most of the doctors and professionals in Panama are black. However, During the debriefing, the leader of the team concluded that Githiga is the only person who can never be a missionary. This pains me, because, I was already a missionary and had participated on numerous domestic and overseas missions. But being analytical psychologist, I realized that that my dear sister was projecting that part of her which she does not like which is known as shadow.

However, those who minister in Christ are connected with the universal power which is both immanent and transcended. Our God is a mighty God He is described by Daniel as:

> "Ancient of the Days: His clothing was as white as snow,
> The hair of his head was white like wool.
> His throne was flaming with fire,
> and its wheels were all a blaze
> A river of fire was flowing coming out from before him,
> Thousand upon thousand attended him
> Ten thousand time ten thousand stood before him.
> —Daniel 7–10

So, whatever you are going through because of your faithfulness and commitment in planting the seed, remember our God is all powerful and faithful. He know what you are going through and will strengthen you. Remember, "no temptation has seized you except what is common to man. And God is faithful, he will not let you be tempted beyond what you can bear. But when you are tempted, he will also provide a way out so that you can stand up under it. I Corinthian 10:13

CHAPTER 25

Conclusion

It is evident that human personality needs to balance between individuality and communality. One should be himself in order that he may make his unique contribution to society. He should be communal so that he may draw from and become a part of the community.

Furthermore, it is obvious that we are fundamentally sexual beings. Sexuality, being vital spiritual energy, generates a loving, warm. and cordial feeling toward one another. For this reason, sex should never be abused nor regarded as a "forbidden fruit." Thus, we need to develop a more positive theology and psychology of human sexuality.

In addition, we have found that we cannot do away with the division of labor since it helps an individual to know his/ her role in the community. However, with the emergence of urbanization, modernization, and professionalism, the division of labor needs to be redefined so that no one is overworked or exploited.

Similarly, it has become clear that we have antistructure and structured spheres. The antistructure realm of our personality is irrational and chaotic. Yet, it is vital since a deeper interpersonal relationship is attained only when the antistructure is reached and appreciated. On the other hand, the structured sphere is orderly, rational, and intentional. We have argued that we need to balance between the structured self and the unstructured self. We should know where and when to be either structured or antistructure.

We have also noted that lostness is a part and parcel of the rite of passage. During the "passages" we may undergo a period of confusion, conflict, disorientation, and precariousness.

The lostness may be either communal or individual. It may have a positive or negative result. We have argued that during the situation, an individual need to be guided and illumined rather than being excommunicated or ostracized.

Moreover, we have seen that pain is a reality. It is evident in the life and teaching of Christ. Pain can either deter or facilitate personality growth. It may lead to faithlessness, inferiority feelings, ego diffusion, self-absorption, stagnation, and despair, or instill faith, hope, love integrity, insight, and wisdom. In addition, we have dealt with the three great archetypal motifs of the psyche: The Tree of God, the Great Mother, and the Great Father. We have asserted that here is the communal tree and the individual tree. The Tree of God connects us with and makes us conscious of our primordial time, the totality of our ontology, and the complexity and ambiguity of our environment. The myths, reality, positivity and negativity of the Great Mother and the Great Father have been discussed.

In counseling, we must first discover our archetypal motifs and find out how we relate to them. As an analyst, we must psychoanalyze ourselves in order that we may be able to psychoanalyze others. We should, for instance, endeavor to discover the phenomena, the objects, persons, and personality types that evoke the archetypes of the Tree of God, the Great Mother, and the Great Father. After discovering our particular archetypes, we should try to discover those of our clients and find out how they relate to them. We may find that the person who has a sick religion may fear to face the Tree of God, which, to a large extent, is symbolized by the holy shrines and religious specialists. A woman who has a sick Great Father may have a problem with or exploit males. A Kikuyu woman who has this problem likes to use a sweeping statement, "Never trust men, for they are animals." Similarly, a man who has a problem with the inner Great Mother will have problems with females. He, too, likes to use a sweeping statement, "Never show a woman your wisdom tooth." Meaning never smile to or laugh with a woman. He may treat his wife and other women as sexual objects. In all cases, the counselor should help these individuals to face and learn to relate to the Tree of God, the Great Mother, and the Great Father since sanctification of life, self-identity, and integrity depend on how we relate to these great archetypal motifs of the psyche. The three are the filters through which we receive the heavenly and earthly grace, which facilitates the movement from glory to glory. The more we allow the water of life to filter through them, the more we grow to wholeness. This growth leads to joy, love, faith, insight, and wisdom.

Moreover, we have insisted that for us to be fruitful, we must be in Christ: In Jesu words: "I am the vine, you are branches, if a man remain in me, and I in him, he will bear much fruits, apart from me you can do nothing. "John 15:5 So in Christ we bear the fruit of the Spirit which is "Love, joy, peace, patience, kindness, faithfulness, gentleness, and self-control. This is the basis of a successful and fruitful family.

Printed in the USA
CPSIA information can be obtained
at www.ICGtesting.com
LVHW061739071023
760448LV00017B/180